Wednesday Adam Story

Wilson Richardson

Table of Contents

Table of Contents — 1

Chapter One, Wednesday's Child Is Full of Woe. — 19

Chapter Two, Woe is the loneliest number. — 53

Chapter Three, Friend or Woe. — 73

Chapter Four, Woe What a Night. — 102

Chapter Five, You Reap What You Woe. — 124

Chapter Six, Quid Pro Woe. — 154

Chapter Seven, If You Don't Woe Me by Now. — 184

Chapter Eight, A Murder full of Woes. — 208

All you need to know about the character you are.

--- You are a Cyborg/Terminator.

--- (Y/N) was born as a human, until her father, a mad scientist, who once attended Nevermore Academy, decided to use her as a test subject when she was younger. Which failed miserably leaving her ingenious forearm to be mutilated, although his experiment was successful, as he made his daughter a robot in the process, which affected her mind mentally and physically, causing her to have heterochromia.

--- (E/C) and (F/C) are your two eyes, you can make it a different (F/C) just make sure it's two seperate colours.

--- NOT TO MENTION!!! You also have a anscestor like Wednesday, but she looks like you but with red eyes, and black hair (it's alright if you still have it, just kind of looks like you in a way)

--- (Y/N) has a device implanted in her head that explains her technopathy powers, the device also controls her personality, actions, and stuff.

--- You are also 17 (Just turned 17) in the book, which explains how she her *restricted* driver's license if you're wondering about that further into the book.

-- The powers she inherits as a Cyborg are:

-- Flight (To fly.)

--   Ability   to   breathe   underwater

-- Techno pathy

-- Telekinesis

-- And also Xavier's artistic abilities.

-- The powers she receives near the end are:

-- **Superhuman strength (Furthermore into the story.)**

-- *Some form of neuroelectric interfacing that allows her to both read thoughts and also give her targets waking nightmares. (Furthermore into the story.)*

-- *Speed Advanced Sensor & Weponary systems (Furthermore into the story.)*

--*Portal Creation (Furthermore into the story.)*

-- *Stamina (Furthermore into the story.)*

-- *Durability (Furthermore into the story.)*

--- (Y/N)'s stepmother is also Marilyn Thornhill, who supposedly fell in love with her dad before he unknowingly passed on a few months after, leaving her in the hands of her stepmother. She was curious about her, but she was often nice to her and treated her like her own daughter, the curiosity fell off her quickly.

--- The many public schools she attended thought of her as weird, and disgusting, which related to her being bullied, which made her father enroll her in the Academy he was in when he was younger, which barely helped. (Since when she attended, she started off insecure and stuff, but she's developing to make friends and stuff, such as hanging out with Enid, Ajax, and more.)

--- Her roommate is Yoko, the two get along and are good mates, but of course, (Y/N) can't tolerate her loud music overnight, as she complained about moving to Ophelia hall, which pretty much didn't work out for (Y/N) since she wasn't aloud too due to Enid's new roommate coming in.

--- (Y/N) is also around Xavier's height, although she's shorter than him by a few inches. (Just giving you an example of how tall she is compared to others.)

--- And talking about Xavier, we also have his perspective in the story, so in my book, he'll be a side character. Preferably one of (Y/N)'s mates.

--- (Y/N) is a chill person, who likes to draw, paint, and do other artsy stuff, and also other hobbies like cooking and other stuff that'll keep her occupied instead of cowering away in her dorm away from others like she used to do back when she was younger. She's much more outgoing now and likes making friends with others once she gets to trust them.

--- (Y/N) also works at the same cafe Tyler does.

--- (Y/N) used to be with Bianca, but the two of them ended it off because it would be complicated for the two to be in a relationship since Bianca's mother was on edge about Bianca dating a girl, so the two of them ended badly.

--- (Y/N) wears the classic black Nevermore Academy uniform, well, technically the blazer. She can't be bothered wearing proper attire as she wears this underneath her blazer, and since her mother is a staff member who's loyal to Principal Weems, she doesn't mind. Being a stepdaughter of a teacher really does come with its perks, (Like owning an art studio.)

That is all you need to know, have fun reading this book!!!

(Y/N) (M/N) (L/N)

WEDNESDAY ADDAMS' LOVE INTEREST

(Insert Picture)

WEDNESDAY ADDAMS

(Y/N) (M/N) (L/N)'S LOVE INTEREST

MORTICIA ADDAMS

WEDNESDAY ADDAMS' BIOLOGICAL MOTHER

GOMEZ ADDAMS

WEDNESDAY ADDAMS' BIOLOGICAL FATHER

MARILYN THORNHILL

(Y/N)'s STEPMOTHER

(DECEASED AT 41 YEARS OLD)

(1981-2022)

(M/N) (M/N) (L/N)

(Y/N)'s BIOLOGICAL MOTHER

(DECEASED AT 30 YEARS OLD)

(19//-2009)

(Insert Picture)

(F/N) (M/N) (L/N)

(Y/N)'s BIOLOGICAL FATHER

(DECEASED AT 35 YEARS OLD)

(19//-2017)

(Insert Picture)

YOUNG MORTICIA ADDAMS

YOUNG GOMEZ ADDAMS

YOUNG (M/N) (M/N) (L/N)

(Insert Picture)

YOUNG (F/N) (M/N) (L/N)

(Insert Picture)

GOODY   **ADDAMS**

WEDNESDAY ADDAMS' ANCESTOR

ASTORIA (L/N)

(Y/N) (L/N)'s ANCESTOR

(Insert Picture)

ENID SINCLAIR

TYLER GALPIN

BIANCA BARCLAY

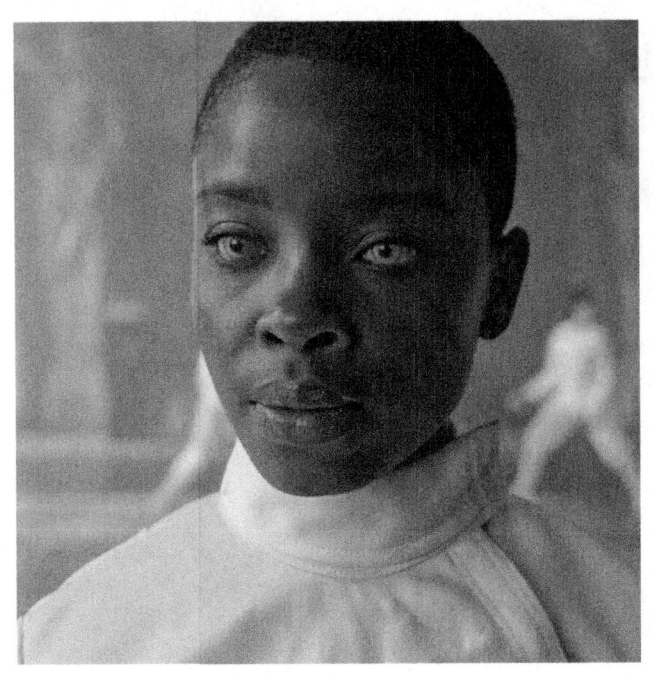

AND MORE

Chapter One, Wednesday's Child Is Full of Woe.

3RD PERSON'S POINT OF VIEW.

The soft clanking of black boots would roam the hallways filled with promiscuous students who dared to stare down at the black-haired girl who had dead eyes, and a look of emptiness on her face, owning everyone's attention, keeping her thoughts to herself.

She gained the eyes of many people, as the bell rang which made everyone leave the area and focus on their daily lessons. The girl, whose name was Wednesday, walked forward to a locker scribbled with black markers which had awful names of her brother, Pugsley.

Opening the locker she stood in front of as she heard muffled noises coming inside, there stood her brother as he fell on the ground. Bending down, she took the apple from his mouth, and with a serious tone she told him, "I want names."

"I don't know who they were, honest." Pugsley begged a look of sadness and terror plastered on his face, "It happened so fast," he whimpered as his sister untied his hands lecturing him that emotions show weakness. Overhearing him Whimper she sneered internally, "Pull yourself together." "Now." She warned as he stopped for a moment, before having a vision of who dared to touch her brother in a vile way.

Once her vision eased, she glanced at her brother for a moment, "Hey, you okay?" he questioned, concerned for her sister as she just stared at him for a moment before telling him, "Leave this to me." She began to stand up. "Wednesday? What are you going to do?" Her brother asked, the sadness and loneliness never leaving his eyes. "What I do best." She responded, taking one glance at her brother before leaving.

The same girl from earlier walked up the stairs to the indoor pool as one of the boys who bullied her brother called her out for coming. They underestimated her, calling her a freak as they laughed at her about it. there as she told them, "The only one who can torture my brother, is me." She began, as she pulled out two bags full of piranhas from her back and let go of them chasing after the boys who screamed in pain and agony, making the young girl smile.

A young girl with short blonde hair with temporarily dyed pink and blue tips was chaotically dancing with energy as a certain raven-haired figure sat on the bed. "C'mon (Y/N), you should join me" The girl giggled as the girl scoffed with a slight smirk seeing her happy over a song.

"I don't like to dance, it's not my nature." The girl admitted making the girl pout, "You're missing out, honestly, Black Pink is everything." The girl began with a wide smile before doing TikTok dances as the girl would jokingly shake her head with a smile. "Oh god, it's raining," Enid pointed out as (Y/N) looked outside, "I like the rain," (Y/N) admitted as the young girl would hum slightly. "The ambiance, of course, I like the soft pitter-patter." (Y/N) admired with a soft smile.

Enid then pursed her lips as she turned off the music sitting down on her chair until all of a sudden the Principal came in alarming (Y/N) as she looked at a young girl with black raven hair along with the two grown-ups behind her who looked at the window full of colors, their smiles fading. (Y/N) looked at Enid puzzled as Enid immediately ran up to the strange and mysterious girl. "Howdy, Roomie!" The girl smiled, as (Y/N) stood up, coming behind Enid, and shooting the girl a pleasant smile.

"This is Enid Sinclair and (Y/N) (L/N)." The Principal introduced as (Y/N) placed her robotic arm on her hip, using her other one to wave. "Are you feeling okay? You look a little pale--" Enid began as (Y/N) frowned her eyebrows slapping her shoulder slightly, "Don't be a di--" The girl whispered-yelled before glancing at the philistine girl with a worried glance, her father then mentioning to the two that Wednesday looks half-dead, which made Enid nod in agreement making the taller girl slap the girl's should making (Y/N) groan in embarrassment.

"Welcome to Ophelia hall!" Enid smiled widely welcoming as she held her arms out about to embrace Wednesday as she shuffled back uncomfortably. "Not a hugger, got it." Enid sadly smiled, "(Y/N) here isn't as well, bummer." Enid sighed as Wednesday's mother then told the two, "Excuse Wednesday, she's just allergic to color," Making Enid alarmed as (Y/N) arms fell on her sides.

"What happens to you?" Enid asked, "I break out into hives, and the flesh peels off my bone." she answered making (Y/N) eyebrows rise up impressed by the girl, nodding unsure of what to say "Luckily, we've special ordered you a uniform," The Principal began as she side-glance down at (Y/N) who was and wasn't in the correct attire making the cyborg sheepishly smile.

"Enid, (Y/N), please take Wednesday to the registration office to pick it up along with a copy of her schedule and give her a tour along the way" She smiled as smiled down at the black-haired girl, Enid smiled giddily as the three of them walked out of the room.

"Nevermore was founded in 1791 to educate people like us." Enid rambled on as (Y/N) followed as she scanned the girl carefully examining her, as (Y/N) was caught off guard when Wednesday told the two that she wasn't planning to stay here at the Academy for long. "Why not?" Enid asked as Wednesday darted her eyes around the room, "This was my parents' idea." She began as she looked at the photograph which had young Morticia Addams standing with a wide smile. "Oh look, there's my mother smiling at me." Wednesday began as (Y/N) chuckled slightly.

"They've been looking for any excuse to bring me here," Wednesday sighed, her eyes, cold. Enid mentioned that there was a rumor of Wednesday killing a kid at her old school which made (Y/N) interested in her, but the girl responded with, "Actually it was two kids, but who's counting?" This stopped Enid from walking, as terror struck across her face which made (Y/N) immediately erupt into a small laugh as she patted Enid's shoulder as shuddered at the thought of being killed.

Enid then opened the large doors, "Welcome to the Quad," She smiled as Wednesday observed the corners, "It's a pentagon." She began as (Y/N) looked at her as nodded, "That's what I said on my first day here too." She began looking at the girl, she did as well. So far the two had a lot in common.

"Those are the Fangs, some of them have literally been here for decades." Enid began, as she pointed out to the werewolves, "Which is dumb." (Y/N) negotiated.

Enid nodded, "And those bunch of knuckleheads are Furs, aka werewolves, like me." Enid continued as she rambled on, "And (Y/N) my dear old friend is a cyborg, which explains a lot. Probably the only one here," Enid spun around, grabbing (Y/N) metal arm as she knocked her knuckles against it. "As hard as a rock, she's the only cyborg here at the academy"

"Terminator." (Y/N) exhaled seemingly, as Enid continued to smile whilst Wednesday observed the area, "And I'm presuming that scales are sirens?" She asked as (Y/N) finched at the name as (Y/N) looked to where Wednesday was staring.

"And that girl, Bianca Barclay is the closest thing Nevermore has to royalty, although her crown has been slipping lately." Enid demonstrated, "She used to date big ol' (Y/N) over here, they broke up at the beginning of the semester, reason unknown." Enid pouted, "Why can't you just tell me, (Y/N)..." the young girl whined making (Y/N) shake her head as Wednesday would look at (Y/N), becoming skeptical. "Fascinating," Wednesday muttered as Enid agreed.

Bianca would then look at (Y/N), her strong blue eyes strucked (Y/N)'s mixed ones making the taller one look at the ground. That's when Ajax, one of (Y/N)'s other closest friends came behind (Y/N), startling her slightly, "Hey, Man." (Y/N) grinned as she fist-bumped him with her mechanical hand, Ajax returning the favor. "Yo Enid, you're never going to believe today what I heard about your roommate." He began as Enid's eyes began to widen as he was giving out confidential rumors about Wednesday, as she stepped back revealing her, which immediately made Ajax regret his choice of words which made (Y/N) laugh slightly as she placed her right arm on Enid's shoulder.

"Ajax, this is my new roommate, Wednesday." The girl introduced as Ajax looked down at her, "Woah." Was all he says, "You're in black and white." He muttered astonished, "Like a living Instagram filter," He began as (Y/N) playfully shook her head nudging him to the side and indicating for him to leave, "Ignore him, gorgons spend too much time getting stoned," Enid told Wednesday. "He's cute, but clueless " Enid admitted, "You know it's a small school and there wasn't much stuff about you." That's when Enid gasped and told Wednesday, more like begged for her to get social media platforms.

"I find social media to be a soul-sucking void of meaningless affirmation." Wednesday began as (Y/N) gasped dramatically, "Damn Wednesday, that hurt a lot." (Y/N) began, as she pretended to act sad making Enid chuckle at her playful attitude, Wednesday would then walk away leaving (Y/N) smiled at the black-haired girl as she disappeared from view. (Y/N) thought that the two will get on good terms.

Enid and (Y/N) would walk back to Ophelia hall, Enid grabbed (Y/N)'s attention after she changed into more fitting clothes, and (Y/N) then placed her blazer on Enid's desk. "(Y/N), I'm going to go hang out with Yoko for a bit, want to come?" Enid questioned as (Y/N) groaned, "Nah, I think I'll just chill in here for a bit, just to read my book" (Y/N) waved the book to her as Enid looked at her for a bit, as she asked her, "What? Can't you read in the library?" "I don't want to hear people kiss sloppily, I'll find it irritating." (Y/N) admitted as Enid smiled, nodding understandingly, "Alright then, I'll see ya in a bit!" She began as she skipped out of the room leaving (Y/N) to chill on Enid's bed as she was reading a Twilight book. (Y/N) then heard the soft clanking of heels come to the door as it opened to reveal Wednesday carrying her luggage. "Oh, hey, Wednesday." The girl waved, her eyes still fixed on the book. The girl just nodded as she looked at the colorful window with a dead glance.

Once Wednesday unpacked her luggage, she then changed in her wardrobe into more comfortable clothes, she then grabbed a butterknife and began peeling the colorful tint off the window, making (Y/N) notice as she struggled to peel the top ones off. "Hey uh, do you need help with that?" (Y/N) asked as she closed her book, proceeding to give Wednesday full attention as she looked at her with a hesitant glanced, and nodded as (Y/N) began walking over to her. "Let me help with that," (Y/N) muttered as she began to peel the top ones off, Wednesday working on the bottom ones in the meantime.

Just then, Enid came in, shocked at what the two were doing. "What the hell did you do to my room?" Enid came storming in making (Y/N) press her lips into a thin line. (Y/N) looked at Enid puzzled. "Dividing *our* room equally." Wednesday began as she kicked the tints over to Enid's side as (Y/N) stood beside her, unsure of what to do. "It looks like a rainbow vomited on your side. " Wednesday began as she walked over to her desk, (Y/N) walked over to Enid's bed, sitting down as the two observed the dark-haired girl. "I--" Enid tried to mutter out angrily as Wednesday interrupted her as she pulled out her chair, her typewriter in front of her.

"Silence would be appreciated. This is my writing time." Wednesday began as she rolled her sleeves up, "Your writing time?" Enid asked making (Y/N) interested, "You write?" (Y/N) asked astonished, "Yes. I find it comforting." Wednesday replied, looking back at the girl with heterochromia as (Y/N) smirked, "I should read one of your novels. I bet it'll be crucial." (Y/N) acknowledged with a menacing smile as Wednesday nodded as she proceeded to write.

"I devote an hour a day to my novel. Perhaps if you did the same your vlog might be coherent. I've read serial killer diaries with better punctuation." Wednesday told Enid making (Y/N) eyes widen as she gritted her teeth, trying not to laugh at the poor girl. "I write in my voice! It's my truth!... It's what my followers love." Enid spoke back, "Your followers are clearly imbeciles." (Y/N) smirked as Wednesday stood up walking to the blonde-haired girl.

"They respond to your stories with insipid little pictures." "You mean Emojis?" Enid questioned, "It helps people express their feelings, I realize that's a foreign concept to you." Enid gritted her teeth as (Y/N) looked at the two, as Wednesday obliged her voice darkening. "When I look at you the following emojis come to mind. Rope, shovel, hole." (Y/N) snorted out a chuckle as Enid glared at the (H/C) haired figure who sat on the bed as she quickly shut up.

"By the way, there are two D's in Addams, if you're going to gossip about me, at least spell my name correctly." She finished as she began walking back to her chair, (Y/N) looked at Enid who had a look of anger and cheekiness on her face as she flicked on her Bluetooth device as began dancing. "Turn that off," Wednesday warned as she began dancing. "This is your final warning." Wednesday began as she stormed up to Enid, (Y/N)'s eyes widened as Enid's nails extended with a slight growl.

"Don't mess with me," She grew as (Y/N) shook her head at the two with a small smirk. "This kitty's got claws, and I'm not afraid to use them," Enid warned as Wednesday's dead look never disappeared, that's when the familiar redhead came in, and Enid quickly put her claws away. "Good evening girls, Sorry about the mud." The older woman apologized as she held onto a flower pot as (Y/N) stood up on her feet, grabbing her Nevermore Blazer.

"Hello, Mother." The girl nodded as the woman turned around her, surprised. "Oh Hello, (Y/N). I didn't see you there," She smiled kindly as she walked up to the two who were standing in the middle, the window splitting the two as the woman stomped her *red* boots, one on each side of the divided room.

"Is this a bad time?" She asked as the two girls just stood there in the middle of the room, as the woman laughed softly walking up to the two. "I'm Miss Thornhill, your dorm mom." She chuckled, "And no doubt (Y/N)'s" The woman smiled as (Y/N) nodded, Wednesday side glancing at her. "Apologies I wasn't here to greet you when you arrived," She began as she looked at (Y/N) who walked to the three, "But I'm sure (Y/N) and Enid have already entrusted you with the Nevermore welcome." She smiled.

"Yes, Enid has been smothering me with hospitality," Wednesday admitted, "I hope to return the favor." Enid smiled, "In her sleep." Wednesday continued, Enid's smile faded as (Y/N) stood next to Enid.

"Well, here's a little welcome gift from my conservatory. I try to match the right flowers to each of my girls and when I read your personal statement in your application, I immediately thought of this one." "A Black Dahlia" Wednesday began as the woman handed the girl the flower pot, "Oh, you know it" Miss Thornhill smiled, "Of course, it's named after my favorite unsolved murder." She looked at it for a second. "Thank you."

The woman kindly smiled, "(Y/N) also helped me pick it out," The woman smiled and Wednesday blinked. "But she was in here?" She raised an eyebrow in disbelief as the woman smiled slightly. "She can just message me through her mind, and I'll just have it on my phone." The woman smiled as (Y/N) nodded embarrassingly muttering slightly, "It's a weird thing I have--" Making Wednesday having a blank expression.

"Okie Doki, before I leave I want to go over a few house rules." The woman began, "Lights off at 10, no loud music, and no boys, ever." Enid and (Y/N) stood there quietly as they looked at Wednesday and the woman continued, "What's the story about going into the local town?" Asked Wednesday, "Passes to Jericho are a privilege, not a right. It's a brisk 25-minute walk or there's a shuttle on the weekends The locals are a tad bit wary about Nevermore, so please don't go making any waves, or perpetuating any outcast stereotypes." The teacher acknowledged as (Y/N) swung her blazer on her shoulder.

"That means keep your *claws* to yourself and no *smothering* people in their sleep." The teacher warned the two as (Y/N) stood there with a slight smirk on her face, internally laughing at the two. "And no scaring kids off with your abilities, (Y/N)." The woman warned as her cheeky smile quickly disappeared from her face, "Oh, it was one time." The girl whined playfully making the teacher glare at her even more, making her stifle a chuckle.

The woman then cleared her throat, "Are we clear?" She questioned as (Y/N) nodded Enid and Wednesday glared at each other, "Well, (Y/N) I'll take you to your dorm." Miss Thornhill began as (Y/N) walked out of the room waving at the two girls with a small smile. "Good talk," The teacher finished jogging up with the (H/C) haired figure.

It was another day at the dismal and enclosed Academy. (Y/N) woke up to Yoko muttering things in her sleep.

Groggily, (Y/N) used her technopathy to see the current time as it was 7:30 in the morning. Annoyed by Yoko's never-ending sleep talk, she decided to get ready and have a walk outside around the Quad.

"(Y/N)." A familiar voice called revealing Bianca Barclay herself. "Bianca." The girl acknowledged, "Long time no see," (Y/N) began as she dug her hands into the pocket of her black pants that comfortably sat around her waist.

"(Y/N), I have been thinking about you lately," The girl hummed as she inched closer to the girl, as the (H/C) haired figure stepped back with a worrisome glance.

"Trust me, Bianca. We know our places, we shouldn't be together." (Y/N) reminded Bianca's eyebrow rose as she looked over (Y/N) shoulder to see Enid skip towards them. "Oh, you hang out with her now?" Bianca asked in disbelief as she looked to where she was staring (Y/N) nodded. "Yeah, I do." She began as Bianca shook her head, turning the other way to walk to her friends.

"Hey, (Y/N)." The blonde-haired girl smiled at the taller one, "Hey." (Y/N) pursed her lips as the two talked for a while until the bell rang. "Let's get to class, (Y/N)." the girl smiled as (Y/N) nodded, following the girl who was a bundle of joy.

(Y/N) dressed in her white Lamés as she grabbed her mask as well as her epee as she walked out of the restroom.

From the distance, she could see the familiar black silhouette of Wednesday as she jogged up beside her. "Hiya, Wednesday." (Y/N) greeted as Wednesday would just stare at her blankly. "Having fun, are we?" (Y/N) smiled as Wednesday just continued giving her a blank look as she answered the taller female, "This is the type of class I enjoy. Challenging people." (Y/N) smiled at her as the two walked together through the Fencing matches, Bianca noticing in the distance as she let out all her frustration on Rowan.

Wednesday noticed as she walked to Bianca as Rowan was down on the ground, defeated. Bianca then took off her mask, eyeing the poor boy."Coach! Coach! She tripped me!" Rowan complained as Wednesday just stared down at him, the coach responded to him in a rough Russian accent, "It was a clear strike, Rowan." "Maybe if you whined less and practiced more, you wouldn't suck." Bianca spat out as Rowan stood up, "Honestly Coach, when am I getting some real competition, Anyone else want to challenge me?" Bianca began as Wednesday told the two, "I do."

Bianca then turned around seeing Wednesday standing next to her Ex Lover. Jealous by the sight, she began, "Oh, you must be the psychopath they let in," Bianca noted.

"And you must be the self-appointed Queen Bee." Bianca agreed as Wednesday continued, "Interesting thing about bees, pull out their stingers and they dropped dead." Bianca's smile faded as she looked at (Y/N) as she looked at the two of them, astonished as she quickly slipped away from the view, "Hell no, I don't wanna be involved in this," She muttered as she sat on the bench.

The two were arguing in the distance as (Y/N) was chilling on the side as the two had a duel with each other, Xavier then walked up to the mixed-eyed girl, "Hey, want a battle?" He asked as (Y?N) raised an eyebrow at him. "You sure, buddy?" She questioned as he nodded smugly as he offered his hand out to (Y/N) and placed her mechanical hand on his as he pulled her up as flicked her mask on.

With an epee in her robot hand, she swiftly and elegantly managed to win out of two matches, until the third round came along, her arm started twitching oddly, gaining self control as she began to sweat horribly, beginning to have a minor migraine as Bianca and Wednesday's duel came forward to the two, Wednesday would then accidentally push (Y/N) as she landed on the ground with a thud with a soft grunt as Wednesday looked behind her stunned, but her eyes widening as Bianca managed to nick Wednesday's head as she pressed her fingers against her head as she looked at the blood, and then at (Y/N) as she used her elbow to sit up, Bianca noticing.

"Your face got that slash of color it so desperately needed." Bianca grinned as she looked down at the black-haired girl before turning around on her heel, leaving the two.

(Y/N) couldn't remember much from there, but according to Enid and Yoko, Wednesday took (Y/N) to the infirmary room, Rowan walking beside the two, but Wednesday refused that she did so. She didn't believe her, and she knows it.

The three of them were sitting down as the two had a conversation, the nurse swarmed the black-haired girl, giving (Y/N) elixir which instantly helped the girl gain back control of her arm, but her migraine never cooled, or stop perpetuating her. (Y/N) used the infirmary bathroom to change back into her clothes she grabbed her blazer and came back and she sat back on the bed as Wednesday did aswell, examining the girl. "I'm just going to tell the nurse something, Wednesday." The girl reasured as she used her hand to wipe the sweat off her head as she walked and then told the nurses that she should be fine and that in a few minutes or so she'd be alright.

When (Y/N) came back into the room, Wednesday was nowhere to be seen, along with Rowan. (Y/N) became skeptical that something was wrong. Flabberghasted, (Y/N) immediately thought something was up as she walked outside, and quickly slipped on her blazer, intending to catch up with the black-haired girl from the distance (Y/N) noticed that one of the gargoyles began moving as it inched off the ledge, "Wednesday!" (Y/N) yelled, her eyes widening, and without hesitation ran to Wednesday with her super speed powers it missed the two from inches as (Y/N) landed on the ground with a grunt, on top of the black-haired girl to see Wednesday's eyes closed.

"Holy Shit, Wednesday I--" (Y/N) muttered as she pressed her hands against Wednesday's neck to check her pulse, as (Y/N) looked up at the gargoyle to see the source of who did this. (Y/N) quickly picked up Wednesday and dashed to the infirmary as she placed her on the soft cotton bed. (Y/N) frantically worried for Wednesday as her arms were crossed over her chest as the black-haired figure sat on a chair beside the bed as she was carefully damping her mechanical arm with a towel, as Wednesday's eyes fluttered open, making (Y/N) notice with a relieved sigh.

"Thank god, you're awake." Wednesday immediately sat up as (Y/N) placed a comforting hand on her shoulder, "Woah, geez, Wednesday. Relax." (Y/N) reassured as she bought her hand back and continued dabbing her drenched mechanical arm Wednesday looked around her surroundings as then looked at the girl. "The nurse said you don't have a concussion, but you probably have a nasty bump." (Y/N) sighed in relief as the girl looked at the ground, and then told (Y/N), "The last thing I remember I was walking outside, feeling a mixture of rage, pity, and self-disgust." She began as (Y/N) looked at her, confused. "I've never felt that way before." Wednesday commented as (Y/N) looked to the ground for a moment with a soft chuckle that believed to be a response to disbelief.

"Y'know... I've never had a fencing match with Bianca before." (Y/N) admitted making Wednesday curious, "But why?" She asked as (Y/N) raised an eyebrow, making eye contact with the girl.

"Because well, I don't like the fact that I have to have a fencing match with my ex, hm?" (Y/N) hummed looking at Wednesday who stared at her heterochromia orbs, as she stared back into her own dark and mysterious ones, making her clear her throat as she then continued, "But then I... I then I looked up and saw that gargoyle coming down at me and then I thought..." Wednesday paused making (Y/N) eyes soften at her for a moment, "Well, at least I'll have an imaginative death." Wednesday gazed into (Y/N) soft, but lonely eyes as she shook her head. "Wednesday, don't think about something as crucial as that." (Y/N) began as she folded up the towel placing it on the nightstand next to the bed, placing her robotic hand on her shoulder with a warm smile.

"You then tackled me out of the way. Why?" Wednesday asked, her monotone voice lacing with curiosity as (Y/N) looked at Wednesday there was a slight glint in Wednesday's eyes, as (Y/N) pursued her lips as she looked at the girl, as she did also. "Well, I wouldn't want to witness someone's death, now." (Y/N) began as she looked at Wednesday she kept quiet for a bit, before stuttering slightly, but her voice was still cold "I didn't want to be rescued." (Y/N) eyes widened.

"You're telling me, that I should've let that thing smash you?" (Y/N) frowned as Wednesday continued, "Yes. I would've preferred it that way." (Y/N) shook her head as she rolled her sleeves down her white shirt, her bust showed as her shirt was soaking wet, her black bra being noticeable, making Wednesday notice as her eyes flickered, glancing away from the droopy-black-haired girl as she slipped on her blazer back on as she buttoned it back up, Wednesday returning her gaze to the girl.

"Are you alright?" (Y/N) asked as Wednesday nodded as (Y/N) offered her a glass of water which was on the nightstand next to her towel as the girl hesitantly accepted the offer, taking a sip of the water. "I'll wait for you outside, hm?" (Y/N) hummed as she then sat down on the chairs outside trying to catch her breath as she held onto Wednesday's small umbrella.

A few hours later, as the clouds cleared, (Y/N) eventually changed into a more appropriate and comfortable attire as she drove in her black 2004 ford-falcon as she was speeding along the highway, getting to the town center in no time, boosting her favorite song as she skidded to a stop.

(Y/N) walked in from the back as she slipped on her beige-colored apron as saw her work-mate Tyler as she greeted him, as he did aswell. "Hey." (Y/N) smiled, "Hey, (Y/N)."

He greeted her as she noticed, "Are you on break right now?" She questioned as he nodded. "Yeah." (Y/N) nodded as she placed her bag down which had a few important stuff that belonged to her in it as she walked to the counter as began brewing coffee for the customers.

(Y/N) was eventually on break, as she then smelt smoke coming from the counter. (Y/N) recognized the smell as she walked out tiredly, "Goddamnit, Tyler you better not have broken the expresso machine again especially now that i'm coming back on shi--" She paused as she noticed Wednesday in the distance. "Oh, hey, Wednesday." (Y/N) greeted slightly confused as Wednesday looked at the girl who emerged from the distance, "Oh, you know her, (Y/N)?" Tyler questioned as she nodded. "Yes, of course." (Y/N) stammered as Tyler looked at his watch, "I guess I should be going," Tyler began as he looked at (Y/N), " Sorry for the machine, you can try to fix it, I guess," Tyler muttered as gave the instructions book to (Y/N) as he walked away making (Y/N) puzzled as she looked as Wednesday for a moment but huffed in annoyance.

"So, Miss Addams, what can I get for you?" (Y/N) began, as she held a worried smile, as she sighed looking down, her smile dropping, coming to realization with herself. "Sorry, Wednesday, I would brew you a coffee of some sort, but apparently the Expresso machine is broken, *again*." (Y/N) sighed, as she continued, "It also doesn't help when the instructions are in Italian." She finished as Wednesday began to walk around behind the counter as she stood next to (Y/N) as grabbed the book of instructions from her. "I thought you could read in any language." Wednesday remarked as (Y/N) gnawed the inside of her cheek, "It can't be helped since... eh, well, I'm not exactly on good terms with using my powers for irrational reasons." (Y/N) commented as she looked at the machine with disbelief making Wednesday nod her head understandingly.

Wednesday then looked down at the instructions, "I'll need a tri-wing screwdriver, and a four-millimeter Allen wrench," Wednesday read out loud making (Y/N) impressed, "You read Italian?" "Of course," Wednesday looked at the taller girl, "Here's the deal," Wednesday began, as (Y/N) shifted her attention to the girl, "I'm going to fix your coffee machine, then you're going to make my coffee and call me a taxi." She finished, making (Y/N) flicker her eyes down at the coffee machine and then at the girl again before saying, "There are no taxis in Jericho," (Y/N) replied, "Try uber?" She acknowledge, "I don't have a phone." Wednesday spoke to (Y/N) as she walked to the back grabbing the materials provided as she came back.

"So like... where are you going anyway?" (Y/N) questioned as Wednesday grabbed the items from the girl as she began to work on the machine, "That's on a need-to-know basis." Wednesday responded making (Y/N) taken aback as she kept quiet for a moment Wednesday then asked her, "What about trains?" "The nearest station is Burlington." (Y/N) recalled, "It's half an hour away." (Y/N) began as she put her hands in her pocket, "You have a valve issue, I've seen it before." She noticed as (Y/N) raised an eyebrow as kept quiet to herself as the smoke finally stopped making (Y/N) grin at her, "Wow, Wednesday. Thanks." (Y/N) thanked as Wednesday turned to look at her, "By any chance can you drive me to Burlington Station, (Y/N)?" Wednesday questioned, her eyes dead serious as the girl creased her eyebrows.

"I'm sorry, Wednesday. I just came on shift, and I don't get off for another hour." (Y/N) shurgged as Wednesday then pulled out twenty dollars in her hand, "Nice, twenty-whole dollars, but still no," (Y/N) apologized as Wednesday pulled out another twenty dollars. "I'll make it forty." She finished as (Y/N) creased her eyebrows for a moment, "Sorry, again. Fun fact about me is that I'm not bought so, it's either you wait or find someone else to drive you." (Y/N) finished as she began making Wednesday her coffee as Tyler came out to the now-fixed machine.

"Alright, (Y/N). I'm going to head out now." The taller guy began as Wednesday stopped him for a brief moment, "Tyler, is it?" questioned Wednesday as the guy nodded hesitantly at the girl, "Yes, can I help you?" He asked as Wednesday instantly said yes. "By any chance can you drive me to Burlington station?" Wednesday asked as

(Y/N) looked at the two in the corner of her eye as Tyler shook his head slightly. "My bad, I don't have my car with me right now, since it's getting done, so..." He dragged off as he then looked at the cyborg girl.

"Well, I'm sure your friend, (Y/N) will sort it out with you." He commented as his bag swung around his shoulder, "See ya, (Y/N), and uh," He questioned, as he had forgotten the girl's name from earlier the girl looked at him hesitantly, "Wednesday." He smiled at her, flashing his pearly whites, "Alright then, Wednesday. See you around." he finished as they walked out of the cafe, making (Y/N) and Wednesday look at each other.

"So, Wednesday, what can I get for you?" (Y/N) asked with a pleasant smile on her face, as Wednesday answered, "A quad over ice," She paused for a moment before uttering a small 'Please' which made the dark-brown girl smile, "As you wish," The dark-brown smiled as Wednesday walked to an empty space, sitting in a booth.

A few minutes after the two had their conversation, (Y/N) was making some coffee for the customers that turned up which wasn't a lot. (Y/N) was busy as her eyes flickered to where Wednesday was sitting as a few boys gained up on her, making (Y/N) notice as she creased her eyebrows, as she stormed up to the three of them, "Oi, you three, back off." (Y/N) glared as they all looked at her, "Or what,

'(Y/N)'?" One of the boys questioned making her glare at them as she gritted her teeth, "Yeah, '(Y/N)' stay out of this." They taunted as she wore a nametag that had her name on it, as Wednesday came forward, "Yeah, (Y/N) stay out of this," Wednesday began as she stepped up to the boy.

"So tell me, freak." He began as (Y/N) was about to go off her rocket until she interpreted, "Have you been with a normie?" He asked as Wednesday glanced at him with her dead look, "I haven't found one that could handle me," Wednesday paused for a moment as the guy flinched when she said 'boo' making one of the guys touch her shoulder, but in an instinct, Wednesday immediately dashed in and pushed him away, as Wednesday would then step to the side as one of the guys accidentally hit the other, as (Y/N) stood there in shock, and as Wednesday's eyes burned with fury, as to what (Y/N) could tell as she grabbed one of the guys and swung them into each other making them knock out on the ground.

And by mere meters, (Y/N) swung her head to the side as her face was about to be impacted by one of the boys' fists until Wednesday came forward and grabbed onto his fist and twisted his arm, as the two dodged his every move until he was eventually on the ground in pain as well as had Wednesday kicked him from the air.

"Damn Wednesday, where'd you learn those kung-fu moves from?" She questioned as Wednesday was cut off by the door opening revealing the chief of the town, "Sir," The girl began as he looked around unsure of what to do, "(Y/N), what the hell happened here?" He questioned as he looked around at the chaos from earlier, "They were harassing a customer, and well, she put them in their place." (Y/N) began as she looked at the chief for a moment, "This little thing took down three boys?" He questioned in disbelief as (Y/N) nodded, slightly impressed by the girl's moves from earlier.

"Did you help her?" He asked as she blinked in disbelief (Y/N) of course denied it as she insisted that this was her doing, not hers. "Where's my son, by the way, (Y/N)?" He questioned as he looked to where the counter as she told him that his shift ended a while ago.

Principal Weems from the school that the two went to came in, looking at the mess Wednesday had made, "Apologies, Sherrif, this one slipped away from me." Wednesday looked at (Y/N) as her eyebrows creased for a moment, "Come on, Miss Addams, time to go." The woman began as she looked at (Y/N) for a bit. "Would you like to come, (Y/N)?" She asked as (Y/N) politely refused, "Sorry, Miss. I have my own car in the back, so I'll--" She was cut off by Tyler walking into the cafe as he jogged beside his father, "Hey, Dad. I didn't know you'd be here." He began, noticing the little conference between everyone as he nodded until he remembered something.

"Wait a minute, hang on." The guy clicked on it as he looked at the girl.

"You're an Addams?" He questioned, "Don't tell me Gomez Addams is your father." He continued as Wednesday nodded slightly, "That man belongs behind bars for murder. I guess the apple doesn't fall far from the tree." He continued as Pluto creased her eyebrows, "(Y/N)'s dad's here is just as messed up as yours." (Y/N) kept quiet as he rambled on, "But (Y/N) works with my son, so serves her right."

"Imma keep my eye on you," He warned slightly at the two left, (Y/N) and Tyler looking at each other with a shrug.

(Y/N) was painting outside as it was quite dark outside, a dark navy blue painting the sky, along with a full moon she could hear a cello, drawn to the exquisite sound she smiled as she walked to where it was coming from as she smiled with an exhale as all the frustration went away.

A while after the anonymous cello stopped playing, (Y/N) gathered up her things and walked to her dorm room Yoko invited a few of her friends over which was normal of her too as she changed into a simple tank top and pants she slipped under her blanket feeling the warmth as she smiled as her friends walked out of the room noticing the (H/C) haired girl with a look of disgust on their face.

(Y/N) smiled as she was about to drift off into a deep slumber until she heard a faint tap on her window which was near her as she became skeptical as she opened up the window to see a hand climb through making her eyes widen as she looked at it as it came running after her making her wary as it went on her desk. She then proceeded to grab Yoko's baseball bat and she tried swinging it as the hand eventually gained control of it throwing it to the side, and ordering her to sit.

It then motioned for her to use her technopathy as it pointed to her head as she looked at it skeptically before its hands opened which had the words written in blank ink,

'CALL ME 4135551938 WEDNESDAY.'

"You could've just asked." (Y/N) shrugged as it pointed the middle finger at her, making her chuckle, slightly intimidated by the hand as it did morse code which said, 'At least I have a right hand.' (Y/N) looked at him in shock as she playfully rolled her eyes with a smile as she used her technopathy powers to contact Wednesday.

"Heya, Wednesday." (Y/N) smiled as a holographic image of Wednesday popped up in front of Thing and (Y/N). "That's Thing." Wednesday commented as (Y/N) looked at the hand, "Is he like, your pet?" (Y/N) questioned as he then pointed the middle finger at her again. "He's sensitive," Wednesday replied, making (Y/N) chuckle once more.

"Anyways, Wednesday, what happened to not being a slave to technology?" She questioned as (Y/N) noticed, "You could've just walked to my dorm, you know that, right?" (Y/N) began as she looked at the girl with a look of dismay as Wednesday remembered, "True. But your dorm is on the other side of the school." (Y/N) chuckled, "Did you find anything interesting in your father's file?" (Y/N) asked with a mischievous grin, "Of course, it was something about this guy, named (F/N) (M/N) (L/N), and also my father, being enslaved in prison for murdering a defenseless man." She continued making (Y/N) eyes widen.

"That's my father's name..." (Y/N) murmured as Wednesday overheard, making her curious, "We should talk about it another time." (Y/N) sighed as Wednesday nodded, she then noticed what the girl was wearing.

"First time that I've seen you wear something like that, (Y/N)." Wednesday commented making (Y/N) slightly smirk, "There's more to where that came from," (Y/N) questioned smugly as Wednesday answered, "Such as?" Wednesday began as she looked at the girl, her voice laced in a playful way, but her facial expression never changed, making (Y/N) eyes widen in shock as it soon softened.

As (Y/N) cleared her throat, "Anyways, it must've been an emergency, considering that your friend-- Thing-- had to come through my window and deliver my phone number to you." (Y/N) began as Wednesday nodded, "It was either you or Tyler." She began as (Y/N) nodded, "Are you still willing to help me escape?" She questioned, "After what happened at the cafe and with the chief and the Principal noticing?" (Y/N) began, "I'm not sure Principal Weems can entrust me out with you now," (Y/N) uttered, "Well, there's The Harvest Festival this weekend, attendance is mandatory." Wednesday remarked, "We're gonna use it as a cover." She then continued, "If you're still willing to drive me to the train station, I can make it worth your while." She finished as (Y/N) looked at her for a brief moment, "Sure. Sure thing, Wednesday." (Y/N) nodded in agreement.

"And, no charge. Consider it a freebie." (Y/N) smiled, "Why?" Wednesday questioned, "Cause, I wish that I was going with you." (Y/N) pursed her lips, "At least one of us will get out of this hell-hole town." (Y/N) finished as she smiled, hanging up the holographic image with a wary sigh, looking at the hand. "I guess this is goodbye, Thing. For now." (Y/N) began as she grabbed the hand walking out to the window, "Bye Thing, Good night, pal." (Y/N) waved as it did also, going away as she closed her window.

It was eventually time for the Harvest Festival as (Y/N) wore a black sweater vest along with a white long-sleeved shirt underneath. "Hey, (Y/N)." Tyler came up to (Y/N) as she stood next to her car as she noticed Tyler. "Oh, Hey Tyler," (Y/N) greeted with a pleasant smile, "What brings you here?" She questioned as Tyler reached into his coat handing her a file.

"And what's this supposed to be?" She questioned examining it, "Wednesday's father's uh-- report," Tyler began as she nodded, "Did she ask for you to come here?" He asked as (Y/N) nodded, "Ah, same here. I guess she didn't think that either one of us would show up," He admitted, as he then overheard his dad calling out to him in the distance, as (Y/N) waved him off.

(Y/N) locked her car as she decided to have a walk around the festival until she saw Wednesday playing the darts and talking to Xavier as you walked up to the two. "Heya, Wednesday." (Y/N) greeted as (Y/N) then greeted Xavier, "I didn't mean to interrupt--" (Y/N) creased her eyebrows as Xavier gritted his teeth together for a moment, "You're not." He commented as he walked away as (Y/N) looked at Wednesday.

"Dude, what's his problem?" (Y/N) questioned, as Wednesday stared at her, "This is trickier than I thought, My mother, Miss Thornhill is expecting me to come to be at the academy in an hour." (Y/N) pursed her lips as she looked to where Tyler was, "And Tyler is having trouble with his dad, I don't think either of us will be available." (Y/N) sighed, placing her hand on her head.

"I've got some dead weight I need to lose first." Wednesday began as the two looked behind (Y/N) seeing Principal Weems. "Dammit, out of all people, she's here?" (Y/N) sulked for a moment as Wednesday looked at her for a moment, "Meet me behind the parking lot when the fireworks start." She began, and (Y/N) nodded hesitantly, "Alright then. I'll see you there." (Y/N) began as she walked to Tyler, with a face full of concern.

"Tyler, will you be able to drop her off at the train station? My mother expects me to be at the Academy in less than an hour, props." (Y/N) began as he sadly shook his head, guilty. "I'm sorry, (Y/N). Since my father knows that well-- you're here aswell as Wednesday, he doesn't like the fact that I'm here with Nevermore students--" Tyler studdered as he looked to the ground ashamed as (Y/N) patted his shoulder, "It's all good, man. I'll manage to drop off Wednesday." (Y/N) reassured as she looked at the time through her holographic lens.

"I'll catch up with you later then, Tyler." (Y/N) began as she walked to find Wednesday as the fireworks began (Y/N) stood near the car park and then saw Wednesday, "Oh hey, Wednesday." (Y/N) smiled as Wednesday hesitantly walked to the girl, "Oh-- And, before we leave, I just wanted you to have this." (Y/N) smiled as she gave Wednesday the file, "It's your dad's police file from when he was at Nevermore" She looked at the girl with a raised eyebrow, "It's from Tyler-- He wanted for me to give this to you since he could come, and I'm sure that it's the reason why his dad hates yours-- and also mine." (Y/N) held a synthetic smile as Wednesday looked at the file, quiet for a moment which made (Y/N) curious.

"You okay?" (Y/N) asked, questioningly, unsure of what to say to the girl in front of her.

"I'm not used to people engaging with me," Wednesday admitted, making (Y/N) smile flashing her pearly whites at her, "Most see me coming from across the street," Wednesday acknowledged as (Y/N) looked at Wednesday for a moment, "You're not scary, you're just kind of..." (Y/N) admitted, "Kooky," She smiled as Wednesday looked at her dumbfounded, before saying, "I prefer spooky," (Y/N) chuckled slightly, "My train leaves in an hour, we're burning moonlight," She began as (Y/N) and Wednesday began walking to the car park as they were stopped by three of the boys from earlier at the Weathervane cafe.

"Oh-- Shit--" (Y/N) began as she looked at her mechanical arm for a moment, desperate to use her magical powers, which didn't work, making (Y/N) eyes widen as Wednesday grabbed onto her as she yelled, "(Y/N)-- We'll lose them in the crowd--" Wednesday began as (Y/N) held onto her hand as (Y/N) used her powers to dash through the crowd as Wednesday accidentally collided with Rowan as her eyes widened as her head looked up towards the sky making (Y/N) notice.

"Wednesday-- Wednesday you alright?" (Y/N) asked as her eyes widened as she looked back at the three boys, "Wednesday-- We really have to go--" (Y/N) looked at her panicked, "Wednesday--" "Rowan come back!" Wednesday yelled, slipping out of (Y/N)'s grasp she looked at her. (Y/N) looked at the three guys before running away in another direction, in hopes of looking for somewhere to hide.

(Y/N) ran in the opposite direction to where Wednesday was she then heard loud blood-curdling screams and a monstrous roar coming from in the woods, curious as to what it was, she obviously ran to the sound, only to Rowan's figure drenched in blood as (Y/N) looked at Wednesday with wide eyes, "Wednesday...?" (Y/N) questioned as her eyes widened at the mess, as his body was clawed, "Wednesday... Did-- did you do this?" (Y/N) stammered as Wednesday looked at her, her face had the same look of terror on it, "I didn't do it-- I swear--" Wednesday's lips trembled as she sat next to Rowan, as then a picture fell on Rowan's lifeless body.

(Y/N) hesitantly crouched down and picked up the picture revealing the two, "What the fuck?" (Y/N) creased her eyebrows as she held the drawing, "That's me-- I mean-- that's *us*." (Y/N) examined the picture as it showed a girl with black hair, as the girl in the picture's eyes were bloodshot red as she was in a protective stance, as behind her showed Wednesday, the background raged with fire as (Y/N)'s eyes widened, along with her mouth.

Wednesday and (Y/N) decided to just head back to the Nevermore Academy after alerting the police, as the police promised they'll take care of it and hunted for Rowan's body. The night was indeed eventful for both of them, mostly Wednesday.

Wednesday was too shaken up by the incident that occurred earlier so (Y/N) took her back to her dormitory, "Sorry about everything, tonight." (Y/N) apologized, "Your plan didn't seem to go well," (Y/N) huffed, "Well if you ever feel shaken up, you know my number." (Y/N) nodded as she was about to leave until Wednesday grabbed onto (Y/N)'s hand.

(Y/N) looked back at Wednesday with a confused glance, "Wednesday? You alright?" The girl questioned as Wednesday uttered slightly stammering, "Although it didn't go as-- as planned. It was a good night though." Wednesday looked up at (Y/N) as her eyes softened, "I'm glad it was alright-- well, for you at least." (Y/N) sighed as Wednesday let go of (Y/N)'s hand.

"Good night, Wednesday." (Y/N) smiled, "Night," Wednesday began as the two bid each other farewell, and with a thump, the door was closed.

Wednesday couldn't help but look at the picture and the police file that belonged to her dad, as she was speculating it, the Crystal ball on her desk brightened up, "Hello my little black cloud," called her father, "So tell us, darling, how was your first week?" Asked her mother, Morticia.

Let's see, she narrowly avoided death twice, discovered that her father may be a murderer, learned that both she and (Y/N) could potentially destroy the school, and was mysteriously destroyed by a homicidal monster.

"As much as it pains me to admit but you were right, Mother." Wednesday began as her dark eyes darted to the crystal ball, "I think I'm going to love it here." She ended with a small smirk.

Chapter Two, Woe is the loneliest number.

3RD PERSON'S POINT OF VIEW.

The next day at the gloomy academy, (Y/N) was quiet than usual, no longer her cherry self, which made Enid skeptical, "Hey, (Y/N). You okay?" She asked as (Y/N) looked at her, then nodded, "Yes, yes. Of course." She nodded as (Y/N) looked behind Enid to see Wednesday motioning for her to come. (Y/N) looked at Enid for a moment, "Hey, Enid. I'll catch up with you later," (Y/N) began as Enid nodded, "Sure, alright then." She smiled happily as she skipped away, and (Y/N) walked to Wednesday.

"Hey, Wednesday." (Y/N) began, as she scanned the girl's face, "Good morning to you too, (Y/N)." She said in her usual monotone voice, as she noticed the girl's eyes and her down-well attitude. "Did you get enough sleep last night?" She asked as (Y/N) shook her head slightly, "Ah, Well. We have a meeting with the local sheriff of the town, Tyler's dad, and also Principal Weems." Wednesday began making (Y/N) scowl annoyed, "Really? Right now?" She asked as Wednesday shook her head. "Yes, of course." Wednesday began as the two made their way to the office.

"How could you miss a dead body?" (Y/N) asked in disbelief, as the sheriff looked at her, "'Cause it wasn't there." He answered her question as they walked, "No footprints, no blood, no sign of struggle. Nothing, nada." He answered in an irritated tone, "My search party looked all night." He guaranteed as (Y/N) replied, "Well your search party is fucking idiotic, they probably didn't wear glasses." The sheriff looked at her with wide eyes for a second before Wednesday came to save (Y/N) from humiliation by the man, "I saw that monster kill Rowan right in front of me." Wednesday began, "I can even show you on my holographic memory card." (Y/N) began. This stopped the three in their tracks, as they all looked at (Y/N).

"Can you really do that, (Y/N)?" He asked, "Of course, I can-- Just let me--" (Y/N) began as forged a holographic screen in front of the three as she tried to think of that moment, "Hold up--" (Y/N) began as she desperately tried to get back to that moment, as (Y/N) eyes widened as her holographic screen fell. "I-- I can't make a 3D holographic image at-- at all," (Y/N) uttered as her eyes widened, as she placed her hands on the side of her face as she trembled, as Principal Weems smirked smally as she turned around, as they all began to walk up the stairs, Wednesday keeping a close eye on (Y/N).

(Y/N) dazed out for a moment until they stopped again, "Sherrif, I find that question offensive," Principal Weems interjected, "I don't care, 'cause I got three other dead bodies in the morgue." The sheriff continued, "Hikers just ripped apart up in the woods." "The mayor said that those were bear attacks" Principal Weems commenced, "Well, the mayor and I disagreed on that." He began, "So you automatically assume a Nevermore student is the murderer, even though there's no evidence a crime was committed." Principal Weems talked back, the man then looked at the two girls, "I'm sorry, I forgot you only teach the good outcasts here, right?" He questioned as (Y/N) looked at him with a dumbfounded expression.

"My guess is that Rowan ran away," Principal Weems declared as they all walked into her office, "State troopers have put out an alert, and I've contacted his family." Principal Weems continued as (Y/N) and Wednesday walked up to the principal's desk, "But they haven't heard from him either," She began, "Dead people are notoriously bad at returning calls." Wednesday was admitted as the Sherrif and (Y/N) looked at Wednesday with puzzled expressions.

"What were the two of you doing out with Rowan anyways?" He asked as (Y/N) creased her eyebrows with a look of concern as Wednesday faked a lie, (Y/N) hesitantly nodding her head in agreement.

"And just to be clear, this monster wasn't a bear or some other wild animal?" He questioned as Wednesday answered his question, "I've hibernated with grizzlies, I know the difference." She interpreted as the Principal put a stop to the two, "Thank you, sheriff. I think (Y/N) and Wednesday are done now." Principal Weems began as Wednesday began, "Actually, I was thinking of speaking to Sheriff Galpin, alone." Wednesday began as (Y/N) looked at her with a concerned glance, "I'm not sure I can allow that." Principal Weems began, "I'm sure I could take her to the station and get a formal statement." He said as she flashed a fake smile, "Yeah let's go," He began as he stood up, "Fine." The woman gritted her teeth angrily, "You have five minutes, and everything is off the record." She continued sternly, "(Y/N). Let's go." She stormed up to (Y/N) and grabbed onto (Y/N)'s arm tightly leaving the two as (Y/N) looked at Wednesday.

(Y/N) was forcefully pressed against the door and locked dead eyes with Principal Weems, "Miss (L/N). You are to go to your class and fulfill your studies." She ordered, "And don't even have the slightest idea of hanging out with Wednesday." She began as (Y/N)'s eyes widened, "Yes-- Yes, of course, Miss--" (Y/N) began as she slipped out of the teacher's grasp as scrambled her way to class.

(Y/N) was consistently trying to distract herself and tried to think of something else, but nothing could replace the blood-curdling screams that she heard from afar, (Y/N) was painting on her canvas in her art studio when the door opened with a loud bang making her frightened with a yelp as she accidentally screwed up her paintings as she gasped dramatically, Enid then came in as the two locked eyes, noticing what she had caused.

"How many times have I told you to knock?" (Y/N) glared irritated at Enid as Enid looked at (Y/N) for a moment, apologetically, "Sorry, Pluto! I swear!" She begged, "It's just that I, Yoko, and the other girls desperately need your help, plus, It'll be a good idea to have a nice breather outside instead of being cramped inside your art studio with the monster you're painting" she mentions as she looked at it as her eyebrows creased.

"I had a dream about it last night, which is one of the reasons why I couldn't sleep." (Y/N) began as she looked down at the ground slightly, as she looked at Enid again as she waited for an answer, "Fine, I'll come along then." (Y/N) huffed as Enid smiled, jumping in the air as she clapped her hands "Okay!!! C'mon now, (Y/N), I'm so happy!" She smiled grabbing onto (Y/N)'s arm as Enid held onto (Y/N)'s hand as they dashed out, (Y/N) making sure that she locked the door.

(Y/N) walked to the boat with Enid as the two were talking about what she could do, as (Y/N) understood a few minutes later, and she sat down on the grass next to Yoko, she then began to paint the boat, which really did help put Rowan's death behind her and make her relax.

A few minutes later as (Y/N) was painting her design on the boat, (Y/N) could overhear Enid encouraging the girls, as (Y/N) flickered her eyes at Wednesday as she was on the other side of the boat as Wednesday looked at (Y/N) aswell, making (Y/N) eyes widen as she looked down flustered as she continued to paint the boat.

Enid then looked at (Y/N) for a moment, "Is it true, (Y/N)?" She asked making her look up agitated, "Wha?--" She said as Enid looked at her, "Is it true that you witnessed Rowan's death?" She questioned as (Y/N) looked at Wednesday for a moment as she lowered her paint brush down before standing up, "Well-- I didn't actually witness his death-- I only saw his bo--" (Y/N) was cut off by Enid as she looked at Wednesday, "As I speculated, you must be losing your mind," Enid began as (Y/N) creased her eyebrows, as she just shook her head, "You know what-- I'll just head back to my dorm." (Y/N) muttered as she was about to leave as Enid and Wednesday dropped their conversation as Wednesday ran up to the (H/C) haired girl.

"(Y/N)--" Wednesday began as (Y/N) turned around her with a hum, "I was wondering if we could maybe explore this odd mystery, together, later on perhaps." She smiled as she looked at her for a moment, "Yes-- Yes, Wednesday. Of course." (Y/N) smiled at Wednesday, "I'll just be in my dorm for a while-- it's a pain getting rid of paint--" (Y/N) admitted making Wednesday nod her head understandingly, "Yes, of course. By whatever means, take your time." Wednesday reassured (Y/N) making her smile lightly, "Thank you, Wednesday." The girl smiled as she waved to Wednesday.

(Y/N) took a long, and peaceful shower as she was interrupted by the mirror cracking slightly making her concerned, "What the fuck--" She uttered astonished as she quickly dried herself up and slipped on a spare change of clothes and uniform, putting her clothes in her's and Yoko's washing machinery room, putting it on (Y/N) walked outside and looked for Wednesday.

(Y/N) wandered around the school, as she looked to where Enid and they were. "Enid-- Have you seen Wednesday?" (Y/N) questioned, "Not since you left, why?" She asked as (Y/N) shook her head, "It's nothing." (Y/N) began as she decided to just walk around and search for Wednesday in the Library.

"Wednesday?" (Y/N) whispered, as she looked behind a bookshelf seeing two vampires fanging each other, which made (Y/N) on the urge to puke, "Obviously not here--"

(Y/N) continued to look for Wednesday until she was cut off by the bell ringing, "At least I'll get to see my mother now." (Y/N) whispered to herself as she walked to her horticulture class, as she sat on the chair, as she bought out her sketchbook, and began sketching out a Black Dahlia using her worn-out thick art pencil.

Wednesday then stood next to (Y/N) making (Y/N) surprised for a moment, "You can sit next to me if you want Wednesday." (Y/N) began as she patted her seat next to her, as Wednesday looked at her hesitantly as she sat next to (Y/N), scooching closer, making Bianca notice where she was sitting.

(Y/N) then looked at her sketch proudly as she placed her hand on top of it, the dahlia sprang out of the book, blooming. "I doubt Wednesday is impressed by your tricks, Miss (L/N)." The teacher began as (Y/N) smiled at Wednesday slightly, "Maybe you are, Wednesday." (Y/N) muttered with a small smile, grabbing onto the flower offering it to her Wednesday looked at (Y/N) for a moment before hesitantly taking it into her hands, "I find it an erratic gift." Wednesday began as she looked at it, "Thank you." She looked, making (Y/N) smile widely.

The teacher then cleared her voice, "Wednesday, we're thrilled to have you join us," The teacher began, "On our journey into the world of carnivorous plants." The teacher walked around in her thick red gumboots, as (Y/N) closed her book placing it in her bag, as Wednesday did the same to her Black Dahlia that she was gifted from (Y/N).

The class continued for what seemed like ages as Bianca and Wednesday would argue over one another with the different types of plants making (Y/N) look back and forth as she eventually got tired of it with a huff until the bell eventually rang.

It was near dusk, (Y/N) decided to go on an evening run to clear things off her mind which worked perfectly, but she could overhear the bells tolling in the distance indicating for the doors to close as she distinctively ran back to the Academy whipping past a few people.

(Y/N) then walked back into her dorm in a huff she grabbed her clothes that were on the bed and presumed to go for a short bitter-cold shower as she whistled while running a shower and then closed the door behind her.

Out came Wednesday, and her friend, Thing. "We need to find out what happened to (Y/N)." She began sternly, as she had a look around seeing art displayed around her side of the room, "Start investigating," She ordered he friend Thing as Thing wandered around the room as Wednesday started flipping the pages of the sketchbook until she eventually came past a drawing of her which made her shocked.

After what seemed like a few minutes, (Y/N) came out of the bathroom, hearing two knocks at the door which alerted Wednesday as she ducked under (Y/N) bed and she then placed her dirty clothes on the bed, she warily walked to the door, (Y/N) then opened the door to see Bianca as she smiled at (Y/N). "Hello, Bianca." (Y/N) greeted as Bianca smiled widely, "Hello there, (Y/N)." She smiled, as (Y/N) opened up the door for her, "You can come in if you want," she offered as she walked in, (Y/N) then sat on her bed, "Do you need anything, Bianca?" (Y/N) asked as she grabbed onto her clothes as put them in the washout.

"Not particularly, I just wanted to see how you're doing." Bianca notified as (Y/N) nodded as she flicked on the washing machine as she walked back to her bed and looked at Bianca for a moment, "However," She began, "I could tell that, well, you're afraid if anything happens to Wednesday." She began as she sat next to (Y/N) on the bed, "Isn't it why you've been following her like a lost-eager-eyed puppy?" Bianca then continued, "Or is there something more?" Her voice laced with jealousy with a mix of curiosity added to it.

(Y/N) then stood up and walked to her open book, as Bianca looked at her, "Seriously, what do you see in her?" Bianca's voice raised up, "You suddenly have a thing for tragic goth girls with funeral-parlor fashion sense?" She questioned in disbelief as (Y/N) sighed, "Bianca, we ended our relationship because of your mother, don't let it get the best of you." (Y/N) reminded, "She treats you with crap, and you can't get enough." Bianca rambled on about Wednesday, "Why are you so fixated on Wednesday?" (Y/N) questioned slightly irritated, "Because she thinks that she's better than everyone else!" Bianca yelled as a few strands of frustration tears rolled down her face.

(Y/N) leaned against her desk, before standing to her feet to look at her with wide eyes. "Hey-- Hey-- Bianca-- I'm sorry--" (Y/N) apologized stuttering as she placed her hand on her shoulder for comfort, as Bianca grabbed onto (Y/N)'s shirt and immediately made the two kiss each other, which made (Y/N) eyes widen, (Y/N) was flabbergasted until the two tore apart. Wednesday looked between the two in shock.

"We were good together, (Y/N)." Bianca locked eyes with (Y/N) for a moment, "Trust me, Wednesday Addams is *not* the girl of your dreams." Bianca began as (Y/N) wiped her tears with her thumb, as Bianca leaned back in as (Y/N) sighed for a moment, before gently pushing Bianca off her, "Bianca, you mean a lot to me, honestly. But this isn't fair for any of us." (Y/N) sighed, "Embrace me?" She asked, her voice cracking as (Y/N) hesitantly did for what seemed like a while.

The two then broke apart, "Goodnight, (Y/N)." She looked up as her hands dropped to the side, "Goodnight to you too." (Y/N) began as she closed the door as Bianca left, going back into the bathroom to brush her teeth.

Early in the morning, it was eventually time for the Poe cup award day, Enid and (Y/N) stood next to each other as the two talked (Y/N) and Bianca locked eyes for a moment, as Wednesday noticed Enid, "We're all set," Enid smiled, "Good, Thing's in position." Wednesday acknowledged, "Wanna tell me what you two were up to?" Enid began second-guessing, "And spoil the surprise?" She questioned which made Enid smile rationally, "Speaking of surprises, your costume is in the tent." She smiled as (Y/N) placed her hand on her hip, "Costume?" Wednesday questioned.

Wednesday walked up as (Y/N) raised an eyebrow admiring the girl who wore a catsuit, "O-M-G You look purr-fect!" Enid exclaimed as Wednesday looked at (Y/N), "Are you not doing it, (Y/N)?" She questioned and (Y/N) nodded, "Yeah, I'm not doing it sadly, but I'll be here to cheer." (Y/N) reassured as Wednesday nodded at (Y/N), Enid then interrupted their conversation, "Only thing, where are your whiskers?" Enid questioned, "Ask again, and you'll be down to eight lives." (Y/N) heartedly chuckled at her inside joke.

When loud fanfare music began to swell in, (Y/N) stood on the dock helping the girls get in until they reached Wednesday (Y/N) offered her hand out towards Wednesday as she paused for a moment before taking the (H/C) haired girl's hand (Y/N) helped Wednesday get in the boat. Wednesday stumbled slightly making (Y/N) eyes widen as she grabbed Wednesday's other hand with her mechanical one. "Easy, Wednesday," (Y/N) warned slightly as Wednesday stared up at her for a brief moment before Wednesday sat down on the boat as (Y/N) bought back her mechanical hand.

Still hand-in-hand with Wednesday, (Y/N) smiled down warmly at the black-haired girl, "I wish you luck, Wednesday." (Y/N) then widened her eyes and pulled her hand back, "I mean-- Yeah-- I wish all of you girls luck--" (Y/N) began as she rubbed behind her neck and looked down at the girls, mostly Wednesday. "I'll be on the sideline, good luck." (Y/N) motioned with a faint smile before leaving.

At the two had their moment earlier, Bianca stared at (Y/N) as she held onto Wednesday's hand, jealously clawing at the back of her mind.

Enid would look at Ajax with a small smile as she waved, "Focus." Wednesday determined as she looked within the crowd to see (Y/N) there talking with one of the other group's hosts, (Y/N) flickered her eyes to Wednesday as (Y/N) smiled at her and waved at her, as Wednesday also, resuming her conversation with the other group hosts.

Bianca noticed, and questioned Wednesday, "What do we have here?" questioned Bianca, "The runt of the litter." Bianca began, "For the record, I don't believe that I'm better than anyone else." Wednesday recalled, "Just that I'm better than you." She finished, making Bianca's eyes widen, as (Y/N) stared from afar as the two argued slightly, making (Y/N) concerned as she came back to the dock standing behind the canoe on the dock.

As Larissa Weems would go on about the Poe cup, how it's one of Nevermore's proudest traditions. It eventually started when she pulled the trigger in the sky, the crowd erupted into cheers as (Y/N) helped boosted the canoe which managed to be in lead for a while as the girls began rowing.

As they rowed, (Y/N) used her (F/C) eye as a telescope as she looked in the distance to see Bianca nod at one of the male sirens which made (Y/N) gasp as she ran past the crowd and to where the mysterious guy stood. She dived into the water, as she only wore light clothes, as she activated her powers which she used to help her breathe underwater, and also glide.

(Y/N) tried not to attract attention as she observed the male siren as he sabotaged a boat onto the buoy which made (Y/N) concerned as she stayed below where the siren was, examining the guy's every move until he managed to make it to Wednesday's boat making (Y/N) alarmed. The boat then made a net covering the male siren as it cried out within the waves of (Y/N). (Y/N) glided through the seaweed trying not to attract any attention from the male siren as it tried to claw its way out as the rowboat drifted the poor siren.

Wednesday ran to a run-down crypt as Enid and the others stayed back, just in case Bianca tried to sabotage their canoe, "See you later, Wednesday!" Xavier yelled as Wednesday approached the Crypt, blacking out as she had a vivid vision.

Wednesday woke up to an area, that looked the same, but didn't feel normal. Wednesday looked around seeing two girls making Wednesday look at the girl concerned, as one had pale-blonde hair as the other had short-black limp hair, wearing a long victorian black dress. The two girls stood next to each other as Wednesday looked at them, shocked.

The black-haired girl resembled (Y/N) in many ways, Wednesday couldn't help but approach the black-haired girl, placing her cold right hand on her cheek, her thumb running down her soft scar which fairly showed, which made the girl look at her with sad eyes. She then stepped back with a hesitant look, gently taking Wednesday's hands down, as fear cowered in her blood-red eyes. "You are the key." The girl who stood next to the black-haired girl whispered to Wednesday as she immediately woke up to Bianca's bickering.

(Y/N) got worried as to why Wednesday's boat stopped, as she was about to come up from her underground hiding place, that is when (Y/N) saw their boat striding across the water making (Y/N) sigh in relief as she followed the boat, that is until they reached Bianca's boat as (Y/N) kept a close eye on the two boats, but at the corner of her eye, she saw a siren come and sabotage Wednesday's boat which alerted (Y/N) as they were headed toward a buoy, (Y/N) came towards the troublesome area as Thing immediately sprang out but was passed out by the male siren.

(Y/N) quickly swam up to the male siren as he was too busy pushing them. (Y/N) immediately punched him in the face, making the guy black out cold as he floated there. (Y/N) then swam to Thing as she managed to catch up to the boat as it drifted back to Bianca's. (Y/N) popped her head out of the water as she yelled out, "Wednesday!"

Wednesday looked at the water, "It's Thing!" She yelled as she gave Thing to Wednesday, as (Y/N) sunk back into the water.

(Y/N) then looked as Wednesday's boat sabotaged Bianca's (Y/N) immediately swam back to where she was before, and ran back to the dock to where people celebrated the Black Cats.

(Y/N) came running back to them as her uniform was drenched in seawater (Y/N) smiled at the team, "Congrats, girls." She panted as Wednesday walked up to (Y/N) and pulled seaweed off of (Y/N) head, making (Y/N) look down at Wednesday with a soft chuckle. "Thanks." She murmured.

The Black Cats stood next to Miss Weems as she announced to the students and congratulated them as she gave them the Poe cup. (Y/N) wasn't there since she wanted to go for a shower, she hated the feeling of sand on her scalp, and it was a pain to get rid of it.

(Y/N) eventually came back from her shower as she stood on the second level of the pentagon, looking down at Wednesday with a small smile, as Enid grabbed onto the cup and then yelled "Whoo!" as (Y/N) clapped her hands, mostly looking at Wednesday, as she did also, "Congratulations to Ophelia Hall!" Principal Weems congratulated as (Y/N) and Wednesday locked eyes with each other, as Wednesday motioned for (Y/N) to come down as (Y/N) obeyed.

"Hey, Wednesday." (Y/N) managed to come as Wednesday muttered a small 'Hi' as she sat next to the foreboding statue that belonged to Edgar Allen Poe. "Are you feeling alright, Wednesday?" (Y/N) questioned as she sat next to the black-haired girl, looking at her with a concerned glance. "Yes. Of course. I'm just not used to crowds." She sighed as (Y/N) nodded her head and Wednesday held onto (Y/N) hand warmly and comfortingly as Wednesday looked up with a confused look on her face.

(Y/N) looked at her confused as she looked up as well seeing a symbol that had a skull in the middle of a flower, the statue was holding in its hands. "What is it, Wednesday?" (Y/N) asked as Wednesday looked at (Y/N) for a brief moment, "It's--" Enid cut off Wednesday as she came to where Wednesday and (Y/N) were.

"What are you doing down here?" Enid questioned as she looked at Wednesday and (Y/N) for a moment, before glancing down at their hands which made Enid come to the realization, "Oh..." She dragged as (Y/N) realized as she quickly whipped her hand back, "Don't think of anything-- We were just hiding--" (Y/N) stuttered as Enid looked at her with a smug and skeptical glance, "Okay then Miss

(L/N)," She said with a noticeable smirk which made (Y/N) look down at Wednesday with a flustered look.

Wednesday looked at (Y/N) for a moment, as Wednesday walked up to (Y/N) as whispered to her in her ear, "Meet me here tonight, 9 pm sharp."

Enid looked at the two with a suspicious look, but Wednesday quickly covered it up by pecking (Y/N) on the cheek Enid squealed loudly as she dragged Wednesday away talking about a ship name for the two, completely forgetting about what she wanted to say earlier as (Y/N) stood there flabbergasted. She smiled slightly waving to the black-haired girl.

"Bye-- I guess," (Y/N) muttered with a hint of disappointment before seeing Wednesday disappear which made (Y/N) smile as she walked out of the cramped alleyway before looking at the statue with a hesitant glance.

Wednesday was typing on her typewriter as she looked at the paper which had the same symbol on it as she put it under her dim-lit lamp, before looking at Enid's alarm clock as it had the number 8:59 pmon it, which made Wednesday grab her things and also, Thing before leaving to go back to the statue where the (H/C) haired girl was sitting.

"Oh, Hey. I didn't think you'd show up." (Y/N) started as Wednesday looked at her dead in the eye, "Do you really think that I'd leave you?" Wednesday questioned as (Y/N) nodded, rubbing her hand at the back of her neck as Wednesday approached the statue with her flashlight, "What are we doing here anyways?" (Y/N) questioned, as Wednesday took out her book and the picture of the two Wednesday shined the flashlight on the paper, making the symbol noticeable which made (Y/N) look at the book the statue was holding, "Oh..." She dragged as Wednesday put the picture back in her bag.

Wednesday then stood up looking at the book that the two looked at earlier, writing the words that were forged in his book. (Y/N) kept quiet, as she looked out for anyone just in case the two were to get caught by any of the staff members, that's when Wednesday tapped (Y/N)'s broad shoulder as she looked down at what Wednesday had discovered.

(Y/N) grabbed onto the book as she looked at it curiously. "An acrostic poem?" She questioned as Wednesday looked at her with a smirk, as she circled the first words from each sentence, 'Snap Twice.' Pluto looked at the statue, and then at Wednesday with wide eyes as Wednesday closed the book, snapping twice.

As Wednesday did, the crow's wings began to flap mechanically as the statue moved back, Wednesday shined her light on it as the statue moved backward as (Y/N) hesitantly walked forward as to her right were stairs that spirals down as Wednesday and (Y/N) walked down, looking through a series of portraits until they reached an open area, which was supposedly an underground-hidden library.

"Damn." (Y/N) looked around, as Wednesday was looking at a dark-purple book. "(Y/N), you might want to see this." Wednesday began as (Y/N) walked next to Wednesday as the two looked at the ripped-out page of the book which made (Y/N) skeptical as (Y/N) helped Wednesday put the book in her bag with a sigh.

(Y/N) continued to look through the row of books that looked like they haven't been touched in decades. (Y/N) darted at the portrait of her father and mother, as they were young, supposedly in his late-teens (Y/N) creased her eyebrows at the unexpected portrait. "Ayo-- What the fu--" (Y/N) was cut off by someone knocking her out along with Wednesday.

Chapter Three, Friend or Woe.

3RD PERSON'S POINT OF VIEW.

(Y/N) and Wednesday's hands were tied together (Y/N) head was throbbing in pain as someone had just recently hit her with a shovel as her back was slumped up against Wednesday's.

The bag was ripped off their head as Wednesday faced the crowd of hooded people, as (Y/N) faced the library. "Who dares breach our inner sanctum?" Boomed a loud and deep voice, "You can take the mask off, Bianca." Wednesday recalled, her eye piercing through the people's mask. (Y/N) could feel Wednesday gently taking off the rope trying not to attract any attention, as the people took off their masks as well as their hoods.

"Wait I preferred you with it on." Wednesday scowled, "How did you get down here?" Xavier asked, "Rowan showed me." Wednesday determined, "Left pocket." She looked at the taller figure for a moment as he walked over to her and pulled out the picture of the (H/C) haired girl as well as Wednesday. "I tracked the watermark to the Poe statue." Wednesday continued, "Then I solved the riddle, as well as (Y/N)." Wednesday negotiated towards (Y/N) as (Y/N) head was bleeding slightly.

"Wait there's a riddle?" The male siren began, "I thought we just snap twice." He began making the other members of the group groan in embarrassment in front of the two girls, "Well aren't you the brightest in the brunch." She indicated to the male, "The Nightshades are an elite social club," Bianca began, "Emphasis on elite." Bianca continued, "We have roof parties, campouts, and the occasional midnight skinny dip." Yoko began, "And Yoko's an amateur mixologist," "She makes a killer virgin mojito. It can get pretty wild." Ajax smirked at the thought, "Wow. Do you guys have a bedtime?" Wednesday asked, not bothered by their heart-to-heart conversation.

"Last I heard, the Nightshades had been disbanded." Wednesday began, "Yeah, the group kind of lost charter 30 years ago after some normie kid died." Xavier commenced, and the group and Wednesday talked to each other, as Bianca wondered, "Question is, what are we going to do with them?" Bianca continued, "Only members are allowed in this library." The group looked at the girls, "I say we invite them to the pledge," Xavier intended, "What?" Bianca questioned in disbelief, indicating on Wednesday, "They are a legacy," Xavier pointed at the two portraits that were together, "After the crap she pulled in the Poe Cup, there's no way in hell." Bianca intended it to

Wednesday, "We say don't go making any waves, she's a tsunami." She pointed out, "Just because I beat you at your own game? Let me save you trouble." Wednesday began, "We're not interested in joining." Wednesday began as her dark eyes collided with Bianca's.

"What about (Y/N)? I'm sure she can join." Bianca began as she looked at the male siren, "Do you really think about joining after getting hit by the shovel by one of your group members?" Wednesday asked with a slight scoff, as the other members looked at the male siren, "Ayo hold on now-- *She* gave me a black eye." He intended as everyone in the room just groaned in embarrassment again.

"Are you seriously turning us down?" Yoko oppugned, "Can you believe it?" Wednesday challenged making the fewer members look at each other, "Untie her." Bianca ordered, "I freed myself, five minutes ago." Wednesday muttered, "Along with (Y/N)." She began as she stood up, and snatched the picture off Xavier as she walked in front of (Y/N), "C'mon, (Y/N). We can go now." She offered her hand out as (Y/N) took it hastily Wednesday held onto (Y/N)'s hand reasurringly as they began to walk near the staircase until they paused for a moment.

"Do you want a matching black eye?" Wednesday asked as she slapped the rope on his chest as the two walked upstairs, (Y/N) glanced at the portrait of her parents for one last time. Wednesday then looked down at the group members, "It's amateurs like you who give kidnapping a bad name." She spoke aloud, sending them a downcast stare before gripping (Y/N) hand and walking out of there.

The two walked to Ophelia hall since Wednesday's dorm was closest. (Y/N) sat down on Wednesday's bed as (Y/N) tiredly and painfully touched her head, looking down at her hand that had a red substance on it. "Ouch." (Y/N) muttered as Wednesday came back with a cold wet cloth, and gently placed it on (Y/N) head. "Hold still, (Y/N)," Wednesday muttered as she sat incredibly close up to (Y/N), and gently patted her head with the black towel which was stained red.

"(Y/N), you should sleep here for the night. Your dorm is on the other side of the school, and I don't trust the Nightshades." Wednesday reassured as she pulled back her hand (Y/N) nodded slightly, her head pondering as Wednesday grabbed her pillow and gently placed her on it.

Wednesday then took off (Y/N)'s hoodie as she placed it on her desk as (Y/N) eyes eventually closed as Wednesday smiled for a split second as she turned on her heel seeing Thing as she glared at him.

She shook her head and began to read the thick book, Thing by her side, as she examined the book, running her painted nails through the jagged ripped page as she reached into her coat and placed the picture on the book as she speculated it.

Wednesday then shrugged it off as she turned off the lamp and sat next to (Y/N), getting ready to sleep (Y/N) whimpered slightly making Wednesday a tad bit concerned as she lightly shook (Y/N) up as she gasped, her eyes wide open, "I-- I--" (Y/N) stammered as cold sweat came down her face as Wednesday sighed softly pulling her in for a hug, "(Y/N). You're safe." Wednesday whispered as (Y/N)'s eyes widened as she tensed up at the sudden embrace, but slowly sunk into Wednesday's arms as the two slept.

(Y/N) eventually woke up to the familiar sound of her alarm throbbing in her head, making her groan as she woke up with a yawn. She woke up to arms wrapped around her, "Where the fuck am I--" (Y/N) muttered to herself as she heard someone clear their throat making (Y/N) look to where the sound was coming from and see Enid, "Enid?" (Y/N) questioned quietly, still adjusting to the morning (Y/N) then realized, "ENID--" (Y/N) screeched as (Y/N) looked to who she was sleeping next to as (Y/N) fell off the bed with a thud.

"Ack..." (Y/N) groaned at the landing which made Wednesday wake up as she tiredly stared down at the (Y/N) haired girl. "You were better off sleeping."

Wednesday groaned as she got out of bed, looking down at (Y/N). "Sorry-- Sorry... Did-- did we uh-- do anything last night--" (Y/N) asked as her cheeks were fuming slightly, as Wednesday sat up and looked down at her, "No, of course not. What do you remember?" Wednesday questioned, "I can only remember-- going down some stairs-- and-- a portrait of my dad-- that's all I can remember--" (Y/N) shrugged, as Wednesday nodded, "What were you dreaming about?" she asked, "Nothing-- it's not important." (Y/N) gulped heavily as she stood up.

"I guess I was rebooting last night." (Y/N) sighed, as she looked at Wednesday with an apologetic look as (Y/N) managed to stand up on her feet. "Well, not to sweat, (Y/N). I think we're heading into town today, cause you know, the Outreach day." Enid smiled as she ran up to (Y/N) grabbing her arm, "And you, my dear friend should go get yourself ready." She smiled as (Y/N) looked down at her, and then at Wednesday for a moment. "Yeah, sure. I'll see you guys at the quad." (Y/N) gave a small smile as Enid walked her to the door and closed it behind her as the (H/C) haired girl left.

(Y/N) walked back to her dorm seeing that Yoko wasn't there, (Y/N) immediately went for a quick cold shower, and threw on her uniform with a sigh, grabbing onto her black messenger bag which contained her books and other necessities as she slipped out of the door.

(Y/N) walked down the stairs as she saw Principal Weems discussing something with the students as she stood next to Wednesday. The Russian coach gave (Y/N) and Wednesday a folder that had the job and the information they were assigned. "Yes! I got Pilgrim world!" Enid smiled as she walked over to the two, "I have natural people skills and a love of performing, so it's kind of obvi choice." (Y/N) shook her head in disbelief, "Goddamnit." She murmured, "I have Pilgrim World aswell--" (Y/N) groaned as Wednesday looked at her's, "What'd you have?" Enid asked, "Uriah's Heap. Whatever that is." Wednesday replied bluntly.

Enid made a face, before saying, "Ew. It's this weird, creepy antique store, you'll love it though." "I'd rather be there instead," (Y/N) whined, "I'm crossing my claws that Ajax and I will be outreaching together," Enid spoke with hope in her eyes as they overheard their conversation with Ajax and Xavier.

Principal Weems then walked up to the three as she spoke to Wednesday, "Wednesday, You don't need to worry about your cello, I'll have it bought to the town square this afternoon." Principal Weems smiled which made (Y/N) blink caught off guard, "My cello?" Wednesday questioned, "You play the cello?--" (Y/N) asked, her eyes widening, "I caught your rooftop serenade the other night.

Impressive." Principal Weems acknowledged as (Y/N) looked at her in awe.

"I also volunteered that you and (Y/N) will accompany the Jerico High School marching band at the ceremony." Principal Weems began as (Y/N) eyes widen in fear, "No, no, no. I--" (Y/N) was cut off. "I'm pretty sure it won't be too challenging to play an uplifting Fleetwood Mac melody, (Y/N)." She sent (Y/N) a downcast stare which made (Y/N) press her lips in a thin line, keeping quiet to herself.

Wednesday and (Y/N) decided to sit next to each other on the bus as they managed to make a stop. Wednesday went first since she was sitting closer to the aisle as (Y/N) sat next to the window seat.

(Y/N) walked to a blank wall and then looked at it as her eyebrows creased, Wednesday walked up beside her. "Why are you staring at a blank wall?" Wednesday asked, "It wasn't blank last Outreach Day." (Y/N) muttered as she looked down at Wednesday with a shrug as they decided to go on a little stroll together, "Anyways, since I can't remember stuff from last night, I assume you do?" (Y/N) asked with a look of curiosity as Wednesday went into her bag and pulled out a thick-dark-purple book that had a golden pledged skull on it which made (Y/N) look at her with a curious look as she flipped to a page that showed the two and the strange creature lurking in front of the two.

"That's odd of us to be in there," (Y/N) commented, with a look of disbelief, "Tell me more." (Y/N) asked, "This journal is supposedly 25 years old. Rowan's mother drew this." Wednesday acknowledged which made (Y/N) nod unsure, "Oh. That explains a lot." (Y/N) squinted her eyes as she looked at the image for a second, "Wait-- what's crack stone doing in the picture with us?--" (Y/N) questioned as she pointed at him making Wednesday look at her, "You know who he is?" She questioned, "Yeah. Of course. That's Joesph Crackstone." (Y/N) began, "He's like, Jericho's founding father." She smiled, "He's like-- a big deal around here."

"Oh, that's him." (Y/N) pointed out at a poster of him which had the words 'Visit Pilgrim World -- Where history comes to life.' Wednesday looked up at the spitting image of Joesph Crackstone as (Y/N) shrugged it off, "But yeah-- I'm not sure of what that means to be honest." (Y/N) muttered to herself before sighing, "We should catch up to the other students-- We're apparently having a gathering." (Y/N) began as Wednesday nodded as the two walked beside each other.

Wednesday and (Y/N) stood next to each other as the two heard Principal Weems announce at the Mayor came forward and welcomed the academy as the two heard him ramble on about things, as Wednesday couldn't help but observe the area, along with (Y/N).

The Principal then waved off the students as they all walked away, Wednesday and (Y/N) locked eyes with each other, "I can tell you later if you want, I'll be at Pilgrim World." (Y/N) smiled at the black-haired girl, "See you, Wednesday." (Y/N) waved off as she disappeared from view leaving the pig-tailed girl all alone.

Wednesday then got the idea and walked to Enid, "Enid." Wednesday began, "Switch Volunteer assignments." Wednesday began as she had her flyer out, "What? No-- Uriah's Heap is definitely not my bag--" Enid scrunched her nose in disgust "It's an emergency. I need to check out Pilgrim World." Wednesday began as she looked at the disappearing (H/C) haired girl, "But Wednesday-- This is not a fair trade" Enid began, "Why would I agree to spend the entire day at some dumpy emporium of crapola?" Enid asked in disbelief, "Because Ajax is volunteering there " Wednesday determined as Enid's mood quickly changed.

"Thing sneaked a peak at his assignment," She began, "But if you're not interested," Wednesday turned on her heel as Enid immediately grabbed onto her hand, "No! Oh my god, thank you. You're the best!" Enid smiled as they exchanged their volunteering flyers Enid giggled and left. Wednesday looked at the crowds of students as she grabbed onto her bag and quickly walked through the crowd and managed to catch up to the (H/C) haired girl. "Wednesday?" (Y/N) asked, "What are you doing here-- You could get in trouble--" (Y/N) asked as her eyes widened with worry, "I managed to swap positions with Enid." Wednesday began as (Y/N) eyes softened in relief, "Oh, that's good. At least we can hang out together today." (Y/N) smiled softly as the two walked to the Pilgrim World.

Tourists would chat distinctively as (Y/N) and Wednesday walked into Pilgrim World, "Welcome to Pilgrim world!" A man declared as the many students eyed the man, "Witch trials every day!" The man continued to yell out to the tourists as (Y/N) and Wednesday came forward, (Y/N) having a puzzled expression.

Eugene would snap photos of Bianca and Yoko as he turned around, "Hey Wednesday, want to take a hummers group photo?" He asked with a smile as (Y/N) looked down at him, "Guess not." He looked down, "Eugene, this is (Y/N). (Y/N), Eugene." She introduced as (Y/N) looked down at him with a small wave, and that's when one of the workers came forward.

"Good morrow, my young nevermore kin." The lady began in a fake accent of some sort, "I am Mistress Arlene. A Real OC." She smiled, as (Y/N) looked at her with a weird look, "Original Colonist." She paused, then continued, "Now prithee, put your cell phones on vibrate and make haste, for you are about to travel back in time to the year of our Lord 1625, to Jericho's first pilgrim settlement." (Y/N) looked down at Wednesday with a slight chuckle since she was a cyborg herself.

The students began to follow the lady as Wednesday and (Y/N) walked close to each other catching up to the students as the lady would point out such things, as houses, different types of establishments, and more. (Y/N) was spaced out for a moment, having an erratic headache, as she could hear Wednesday ask the woman something (Y/N) fell on the ground with a thud, ending up in a dark and dismal place, her headache, never-ending.

"The fuck am I?--" (Y/N) questioned as she stood up uneasily as looked around the dark void, that's when an eerie voice muttered beside her ear. "Save her." (Y/N) gasped as she turned around seeing a vivid image of her, but with black hair and saddened red eyes fading distinctively, standing next to a pale blonde girl with dark eyes, placing her hand on the spitting image of (Y/N). (Y/N)'s eyes widened in fear as the ground below her shattered making her drop in as she felt like drowning but immediately woke up to the blinding light that scorched from the sun.

Wednesday shook her up, with a worried look on her face as the woman looked down at her with a slight scowl on her face. "Ma'am, the class is right over there near that cafe." The woman pointed, "I suggest you follow them." She gritted her teeth as (Y/N) groaned, sitting up as Wednesday placed a comforting hand on her shoulder.

(Y/N) managed to stand up with the help from Wednesday, "Thanks, Wednesday." (Y/N) muttered, "Are you still injured from last night?" Wednesday asked, with a worried expression, "No-- No... I'm fine, I just blacked out for a moment." (Y/N) sighed as the two walked to where the lady held uniforms as the two stood next to Eugene.

Wednesday grabbed a uniform with an expressionless look again, "Are these for muzzling tourists?" The lady just looked at her and then at (Y/N) as she rolled her eyes at the two girls.

"It's too fucking small." (Y/N) complained as she held her breath, struggling to put the uniform on "It's the biggest one, (Y/N)." Wednesday reassured as she helped (Y/N) pull down her dress, "God-- It hurts--" (Y/N) began as Wednesday patted (Y/N) shoulder. "We managed to get it on at least." Wednesday acknowledged as (Y/N) sighed.

"I'm not cut out for this." (Y/N) began as she stepped down the stool, as Wednesday looked at her, "It's quite alright. We should do our jobs though. Mistress Arlene is already mad at us." Wednesday began as she looked down at (Y/N) long-black-victorian dress. "Yeah. Lets." (Y/N) began as the two of them walked out, as Wednesday was handed a tray and was motioned to go stand near the corner of the cafe, whilst (Y/N) was ordered to stand next to the door and welcome people in.

As a few minutes went by, (Y/N) glanced in the direction of where Wednesday was standing, as a few tourists were looking at her as she spoke in a german accent, making the people feel engaged as (Y/N) flickered her eyes at her in awe then the people left, making (Y/N) snap out of it as she waved to them goodbye as the woman came back looking at Wednesday, as she flashed her a small smirk.

Wednesday negotiated for (Y/N) to follow her as she looked at the lady for a moment, as Pluto was about to leave. "Hey. watch it, young lady." She warned with a frightening look as (Y/N) looked at her, "Sorry-- sorry..." She apologized as she walked past the lady, in hopes of finding Wednesday.

(Y/N) looked everywhere until she eventually saw Eugene awkwardly standing where the meeting house was being renovated (Y/N) walked up to him, "Heya Buddy-- Have you seen Wednesday?" She asked, her eyes darting around the area, as he studdered lightly, "I-- I haven't seen her anywhere (Y/N)--" He began as (Y/N) looked at him with a certain look.

"She's in there, isn't she?" She began as his eye's widened as (Y/N) patted his shoulder, "Don't worry, I won't tell anyone." She acknowledged as she walked in there, "Heya Wednesday--" Wednesday was staring at the tall mannequin which resembled Joesph Crackstone which made (Y/N) eyes slightly widen.

"Damn-- He's tall--" (Y/N) muttered as the door closed behind her as she walked next to Wednesday, as she felt a small tug on her leg from Thing, as he pointed at the portrait. The two walked to the painting, carefully examining it. "The old meeting house, 1625" Wednesday read out loud, as (Y/N) looked at the canvas, to see the sickening image of herself and also a girl with pale-blonde hair behind her.

The black-haired girl with darkening red eyes had her hand on the girl's shoulder, and the two looked at the painting with a dark, but serious look.

"What the fuck..." (Y/N) whispered breathlessly as her soft fingertip brushed over the canvas, which had the girl that looked exactly like her. "Thing-- These are the girls from my vision--" Wednesday began with wide eyes, as (Y/N) did also. "I-- I should say the same aswell--" (Y/N) muttered, examining the girl, "But... Who is she?" (Y/N) pointed out, "She's even holding the same book..."

Wednesday muttered as (Y/N) eyes flickered to the pale blonde-haired girl, "The same book she was holding outside Crackstone's crypt." She began as (Y/N) eyes widened.

(Y/N) and Wednesday then looked at each other with the same disturbing look, "Are we being haunted--" (Y/N) asked, terrified. "Of course not-- At least I don't believe so." Wednesday glanced around until she saw an old decaying black book, behind thin glass. "This is the book." A small smile tugged at her lips which made (Y/N) notice as she opened the glass case, retrieving the book.

"Codex Umbraum." She muttered, examining the book, "That's Latin for Book of shadows." (Y/N) pointed back, using her technopathy powers, as Wednesday nodded, as she began to flip the pages which were obliviously blank, making (Y/N) notice as she walked next to Wednesday. "Great. It's a fake." Wednesday began as she looked behind the book, as it showed a barcode at the back.

"I don't know who Etsy is, but I doubt she was an outcast settler." Wednesday shook her head as (Y/N) felt like someone was about to come in.

(Y/N) acted quickly as she gently, but swiftly closed the glass case, placing Wednesday on it as she still held onto the book, but her eyes widen at the (H/C) haired girl, as she gently smudged her lipstick with her thumb, as looked at Wednesday apologetically, as (Y/N) pulled Wednesday in, their bodies, close together.

Just then the door immediately flung open, the woman gripping onto Eugene's shirt. "Just what the fudge are you doing in here, missy--" The woman was caught off guard by the two embracing each other as (Y/N) sent the woman a side glance. "Mistress Arlene. How now?" (Y/N) questioned. The woman was too stunned to speak but managed. "How now indeed." She regained her posture, "I proclaimed the meeting house is under repair." She gritted her teeth, "I know thoust heard me."

"I told her the door was unlocked, and you were dying to learn more about Crackstone." Eugene began as (Y/N) shook her head at him, glancing down at Wednesday, who was a mess. "And I come in here too-- too-- you girls--" The woman began, stuttering. "Either way, that book's a replica." "You don't say." Wednesday glared, "The original was stolen last month during the two o'clock witch trial." The woman sighed, still glaring at the two. "It was probably the only authentic thing you have in here, yet you still charge $29.95 a ticket?" (Y/N) managed, as she glared at the woman.

"Hold thy tongue." She demanded, "I'm reassigning you three." She scoffed, crossing her arms. "To fudge-churning duty." She began, looking down at the three with a scowl. "The original meeting house, where is it?" Wednesday questioned, "How the hell should I know?" The woman flickered her eyes slightly, "I only moved from Scottdale in April." The woman admitted. The woman paused for a moment, "Now hurry up, we best be going." She began, walking out along with Eugene as (Y/N) looked at Wednesday for a moment.

"Sorry Wednesday-- I didn't mean for you to be put in this position--" (Y/N) apologized as she helped Wednesday get down with an apologetic look. "It's fine. At least we didn't get in trouble." Wednesday nodded understandingly as (Y/N) gently lifted up her face, using her thumb to gently get the Lipstick that smudged on her face.

"There we go." (Y/N) smiled as they could hear the woman yell for the two to get out, which alarmed the two as Wednesday grabbed Thing and put him in her bag as they left.

(Y/N) and Wednesday were once again separated from one another, but Wednesday had the slightest idea to go to Tyler for some help since the two talked to each other most of the time, so (Y/N) was left alone. Ever since the incident in the fraud-old meeting house, Wednesday hadn't spoken to her since then.

Wednesday ventured to the run-down old meeting house with the help of Tyler and he willingly help her, as she entered in, she placed down her bag as Thing sprawled out from it. "I was expecting more too." Wednesday admitted until appeared out of nowhere, a man with a scraggly beard taunted behind her, "Who you talking to, little girl?" Wednesday turned around, looking at the man.

"Use 'Little' and 'Girl' to address me again and I can't guarantee your safety." Wednesday warned slightly, as the man began to fume in anger, "This is my place, get out!" he yelled, "Thing, a hand here?" She looked down at the hand, which made the man horrified, as Thingy immediately crawled up on him, freaking out he ran away.

Thing crawled back to Wednesday, asking if she were to have a vision which she declined. "My visions happen spontaneously," She began as Thing motioned her to contact her mother, "I'd rather dye my hair pink than ask my mother." She shook her head, Thing then told her to touch an object that could somehow help her vision. "Oh? Want me to prove it to you?" She scoffed as she placed her hand on the decaying wood, and then on the walls of the house that barely stood there.

"Nothing." She muttered, looking at Thing. "Ah, I bet this will give us some real insight." Wednesday began sarcastically as she held onto a brown paper bag that had the words Taco bell on it as she twitched her head, acting like she were to have a vision. "My visions are about as predictable as shark attacks," she muttered grabbing onto her bag as she was to exit through the doors of the house, as she were to exit the house, her palm rested upon the door as she had another vision, falling into the past.

She fell on her knees in shock, as the whole scenery changed into people clamoring, "GOODY!!!" A girl yelled fearfully as she rushed past Wednesday, tripping on her feet as she continued to run to her. Wednesday glanced up at the black-haired girl who zipped past her as the girl immediately went to the people that surrounded the girl as pushed her around, taunting her.

"Get your hands off her!" The girl hissed as Wednesday hid behind the barrell in fear, looking at the girl trying to get within the crowd as she was immediately flung back as she was jabbed to her side by a pitchfork making her scream in pain as she reached out to the pale-blonde girl that Wednesday could see in the distance.

The girl's pain immediately went into pure rage. The girl immediately ripped the pitchfork from her side which intimately clawed her insides. She managed to transform into a bat, elegantly flying over them as she stood in front of Goody. "Don't you *dare* touch her!" The girl yelled standing in a protective stance as she stood in front of Goody Addams, her fangs showing, and her claws showing as her deep red eyes glowed in the dark her eyes will fill with fury and rage, as Goody stood behind the mysterious girl in fear as she held onto the taller girl's shoulder in fear, trembling as the villagers stepped away in fear of the girl.

"STAND ASIDE!" A man's voice yelled, making Wednesday's eyes flicker to the man in curiosity, as the man stepped aside, showing a man which resembled Joesph Crackstone. "Goody Addams! And Astoria (L/N)!" The man yelled, as the girl, glared at him, "You girls have been judged before God and found guilty." The man seethed, "You are a witch," He pointed to Goody Addams, "And you, are a VAMPIRE!" He yelled as Astoria looked at him in rage

"Lucifer's mistress herself." He spat on the ground with a scowl as Astoria's eyes widened, "Who gave you the right to judge one's actions, as you cannot see your own!" Astoria yelled as the man scoffed at her, "For your sins, you both shall burn this night, and suffer the flames of eternal hell." He began as Astoria's eye's widened, "Goody Addams is innocent!" Astoria remarked, "It is you, Joesph Crackstone, that should be tried!" The young girl hissed, her fangs showing, "We were here before you." Goody's voice trembled, beginning to step forward. "Living in harmony with nature and the native folk." Goody began, coming forward angrily.

"But you have stolen our land!" The girl yelled, "You have slaughtered the innocent, you have robbed us of our peaceful spirit." Goody Addam's reasoned, "You are the true monsters." She gritted her teeth, "All of you!" She yelled as she drew out her knife, proceeding to slit his face, as the villager people began to straddle the two girls, as the man touched his face.

"The Devil ne'er sent such a demon. And I will send you back!" He began as he slapped Goody Addams harshly which made Astoria's eyes burn with hatred for the man, "You fucking cunt!" The girl yelled as she kicked him hard, managing to push him back as she was still straddled by the villagers. "No-- No!" Goody Addams cried out as the man, Joesph Crackstone angrily grabbed the knife Goody held as he stabbed her in her heart, making Astoria's eyes widen in pain, making her gasp.

The two were then hollered into the house, Wednesday quietly slipping in. "You are abominations in the Devil's grip!" The man yelled, throwing the two on the ground.

"Astoria!" the girl yelled as she cradled the dying girl in her arms Astoria's eyes widened in fear, looking at Goody, the noise being distinctive for the two as they only looked at each other in fear, the only sound audible was the door slamming shut.

"No-- no, no, no, no--" Goody panicked as she looked at Astoria for a moment, "Please-- please--" She begged as she pulled the knife from Astoria's heart and applied pressure onto it. "Breathe, Astoria-- Breathe--" Goody panicked as she quickly ran to her parents, the house immediately began to blaze on fire. Astoria hastily limped over to Goody and her parents. "Run! Avenge us!" The woman begged, "Find the others, and save our future." The woman would cough as Astoria placed her hand over her heart as used her other to place on Goody Addams' shoulder.

"Please! My sweet lamb," The woman begged, "Run! Run as fast as you can, and help Astoria!" The woman cried out, "You two are our only hope!" The woman cried out as the girl nodded, turning to Astoria "Astoria--" Goody mumbled looking at Astoria with sad and pained eyes. "Goody-- We must flee--" The black-haired girl muttered, gripping her heart in pain and making her wince. "We'll be free, I promise." Astoria promised as Goody nodded, grabbing onto Astoria as the two looked for an exit, Astoria's arm over Goody's shoulder as the two ripped the floors apart under the carpet the two quickly made an escape, Goody closing the door behind.

The area then faded into a cold and damp foggy area, as Goody and Astoria ran, which alerted Wednesday.

"He won't stop until he's killed us all!" Goody Addams pleaded as she ran up to Wednesday, gripping her shoulders, she then gasped as she looked behind Wednesday. "He's here..." Astoria uttered a whisper as she grabbed onto Goody's hand, as Wednesday turned behind her seeing Crackstone's menacing smile.

"There will be no escape for you." He smiled menacingly.

Wednesday woke up on the ground gasping for air.

Wednesday got up in shock as she trembled, her hands shaking as she was drenched in dirt, as her clothes were cold and damp. "Thing-- I saw her--" Wednesday began, "The girl from my visions." She paused for a moment, "The girl from my visions..." She repeated, as Thing looked at her weirdly, as Wednesday looked down at Thing in worry, She began, looking down in disbelief, "Was Goody Addams--" Wednesday muttered.

"And the other one..." She paused looking down at Thing as she scooped him up in her hands, "Was Astoria (L/N)" She whispered with a faint smile, as Thing looked at her, with a weird look, but stayed quiet. "She's (Y/N)'s ancestor." She looked at him, guaranteed. "I'm not too sure though." Wednesday shrugged, unsurely as she looked down at Thing and let him go for a moment until she heard a strange noise as she stepped towards the door that she touched earlier, as she peeked behind the door unnervingly. "It must've been the bearded man from earlier." Wednesday proclaimed as she looked down at Thing as she looked back through the run-down door seeing the same creature as it looked at her through it as it snarled, making her gasp.

"Cmon-- Cmon!" Wednesday yelled as she grabbed onto Thing and her bag and immediately ran out of there, following the monster; but as she was walking, she noticed the monster's tracks as it went from a monster to human footprints. "The monster's human." Wednesday began examining the footprints.

"Wednesday-- I--" (Y/N) began trying to catch her breath, "I'm sorry-- I--" (Y/N) panted as she paused and looked down at Wednesday for a moment as she kept quiet. "What are you doing?--" (Y/N) asked as she held onto her umbrella over the two. "I was following the monster." Wednesday began, looking at (Y/N) for a moment, "You saw it?" She asked, "It's here?-- Do you have a death wish or something--" (Y/N) panicked as she grabbed onto Wednesday's hand.

Wednesday then paused, hesitantly retrived her hand back, asking (Y/N), "What are you doing here?" She questioned, "I went to Xavier to ask where to find you-- and he mentioned that you were wanting to go to the old meeting house or something--" (Y/N) began and paused slightly, "And Mistress Arlene was also wondering where you-- so I went to Xavier-- and then I suddenly blacked out-- I remembered something-- Like a lost memory or something--" (Y/N) muttered under her breathe, "But thankfully I didn't end up in a hospital or something--" (Y/N) chuckled dryly at her joke. "But uh yeah." (Y/N) ended. "I did learn something." Wednesday began, looking up at (Y/N).

"The monster's human." (Y/N)'s eyes widened for a moment in shock, "Its tracks turned from monster prints to human ones." Wednesday commented as she looked down at the muddy ground, (Y/N) followed her gaze, and the two walked as the rain already washed it away. "Damn." (Y/N) breathed out, "The rain washed them away." Wednesday looked down in disappointment, looking back at (Y/N), she then placed her mechanical hand on her shoulder. "It's alright, Wednesday. We'll track that monster someday." She sighed, as the two walked close together quietly.

"What do you remember, anyways?" Wednesday began as she side-glanced at (Y/N) as looked down at the ground, creasing her eyebrows. "I can only remember, well, blinding lights-- like fire-- *bloodshot eyes.*" (Y/N) muttered, trying to recall as Wednesday looked at her intrigued, "Sorry-- Sorry..." She began, "It's pretty embarrassing--" (Y/N) muttered, "No-- No, of course not-- No need to worry." Wednesday reassured, "Tell me more," She began as she raised an eyebrow.

"Well-- I remember that girl's from that portrait we saw earlier, that-- Aria-- or was it Astronaunt-- Ack-- I forgot her name--" (Y/N) tried to remember, as Wednesday's ears perked up, "Astoria... You mean Astoria, right?" Wednesday began looking at (Y/N) slightly as they walked, the two walked close to each other. "Yes, that was her name. Thank you." (Y/N) thanked her as she continued, "That girl-- Astoria. She reminds me of someone." (Y/N) paused, "Do you think it means something?" (Y/N) questioned, looking down at Wednesday, eyes filled with curiosity.

"Not quite." Wednesday muttered, her voice croaked as (Y/N) shrugged, digging her hand in her pocket as she other held the umbrella up as they continued to walk. "Either way, I believe Rowan is right." Wednesday began, "Something bad is going to happen, and I need to stop it." Wednesday began, "Starting with the monster." She stopped making (Y/N) stop as look at her, "Whoever it is." She glared at (Y/N) for a moment before walking ahead making (Y/N) crease her eyebrows as she followed Wednesday behind.

The weather eventually cleared up as (Y/N) sat on the white piano which was borrowed from the local high school, that had exquisite black and gold designs on it as she was handed a piano sheet from Principal Weems as she thanked her.

(Y/N) could then see Wednesday at the corner of her eye as she looked upon the tall statue of the madman himself, Joesph Crackstone. (Y/N) looked at her warily as she shrugged, and opened up the piano, placing the following piano sheets on the stand.

(Y/N) sat near the group, behind Wednesday as she waved at Wednesday, as Wednesday's eyes flickered at her for a moment she just looked down and opened her case to her Cello which made (Y/N) concerned for her as she looked down at the piano keys as the Mayor and Principal Weems were talking amongst themselves to the Nevermore and Jericho students.

(Y/N) was daydreaming when she realized that the bands were playing as she quickly began to go with the flow as they were playing 'Don't Stop' by Fleetwood Mac. Her fingers elegantly danced along the keys as Bianca admired her from the distance, (Y/N) noticed and sent her a small and warm smile as a few people snapped photos of the Principal and the Mayor themselves, as he pressed a button allowing water to come out of the fountain which had Joesph Crackstone on it which made the crowd cheer.

Wednesday noticed the interaction between both (Y/N) and Bianca as she looked at Thing and nodded towards him as he lit up a match, proceeding to light up a trail of gasoline that led to the fountain, making some of the people notice.

As (Y/N) sent Bianca a small-warm smile, (Y/N) could smell the faintest smell of gasoline and smoke which made her curious as she looked behind her, never taking her keys off of the Piano, that is until all of a sudden, a loud booming noise could be heard which made her yelp and stand up in shock, making her knock the chair over.

Many people screamed as (Y/N) stood there with wide eyes as many people screamed and evacuated. (Y/N) looked down at Wednesday with a small smirk, "You did this, huh?" (Y/N) remarked as Wednesday just looked at her with a small smirk of her own as she began to strum a few notes on her Cello which made (Y/N) grab her chair which fell as she sat up on it as Wednesday began to intensely play 'Vivaldi's Winter' on the Cello as (Y/N) followed along aswell which made Wednesday smile as the people ran and scrambled out of the area, and (Y/N) and Wednesday continued to play their instruments, although, on the other hand, the adults were not impressed by their course of actions.

(Y/N) and Wednesday were eventually in the Principal's office.

"That was a disaster!" Principal Weems paced back and forward and (Y/N) hung her head down in shame, "The Mayor is furious!" The woman yelled, "I've lost count of the angry phone calls, emails, and people in town, alumni, parents" She yelled pointing at the two with a dead serious look, "They want answers and so do I!" She yelled which made (Y/N) jump slightly at the loud voice.

"I would lead the inquisition, but I left my thumbscrews and rack at home." Wednesday handled the situation as (Y/N) kept quiet to herself. "The both of you are already on thin ice." The woman has shaken up angrily, "Wafer-thin ice." She scowled at the two, "I swear on my late scorpion's soul, my hands are clean." Wednesday then paused looking at (Y/N) who was both scared and nervous, "Her's too." She reassured.

"I may not have hard evidence but I see you." She scowled at Wednesday, "The both of you." She looked at (Y/N) which made her look down in sadness. "You both are trouble magnets." She glared down at the two, "If trouble means standing up to lies, decades of discrimination, centuries of treating outcasts like second-class citizens, or worse." Wednesday stood up and walked over to the Principal standing in front of her.

"What are you talking about?" The woman questioned as (Y/N) went to go stand beside Wednesday with an unsure look, "Jericho." (Y/N) muttered, "Why does this town even have an Outreach day?" (Y/N) questioned, "Don't you know its real history with outcasts?" Wednesday questioned aswell as the two looked at each other for a moment, then at the Principal.

"The *actual* story of Joesph Crackstone?" Wednesday questioned raising an eyebrow at her as the woman looked down at her as the woman admitted, which made (Y/N) scoff as Wednesday questioned once more, "Then why be complicit and cover it up?" She questioned, "Those who forget history are doomed to repeat it." Wednesday acknowledged.

The two continued to bicker about opportunities and dooms as (Y/N) couldn't get that heavy feeling off her chest until eventually, they were free to go.

(Y/N) and Wednesday didn't talk to each other or spare each other a Goodnight and such as (Y/N)'s mind was clouded as she decided to paint the monster she keeps seeing in her dreams in her art studio.

As she painted the monster, a claw sprang out of the painting which made her gasp in pain as she held onto her neck in pain as it bled poorly. The claw went back into the painting as if nothing happened. She immediately had enough and walked out of there as the blood came down her back, feeling a pang of guilt as she didn't get the chance to talk to Wednesday.

(Y/N) immediately grabbed chains as she locked her art studio, walking away and wincing in pain.

Chapter Four, Woe What a Night.

3RD PERSON'S POINT OF VIEW.

Wednesday decided to head over to Jericho's local mortuary along with Thing to examine the amputated bodies as they were mere seconds from getting caught, but eventually got out of there with sick evidence, photos if you may.

Wednesday eventually made it back as she talked to Enid until she finally fainted.

Wednesday and Thing looked at each other as her body lay down on the ground. (Y/N) knocked on the door as she opened it revealing Enid on the floor, "Sorry for the intrusion I think I left my other hoodie in here--" (Y/N) opened the door as she looked down at the ground and then at Wednesday. "Damn." (Y/N) groaned as she opened the door widely stepping into the room with a small sigh.

"What'd she faint to this time?" (Y/N) raised an eyebrow, placing her mechanical hand on her hip and looking down at the poor girl. Wednesday looked at (Y/N) as she waved her over to where she stood as (Y/N) hesitantly walked to Wednesday examining her large pictures of amputated organs or body parts.

(Y/N) took one of the photos in her hand as she looked at them as Wednesday went on about them. "So, where'd you get 'em from?" (Y/N) asked, "Somewhere." Wednesday muttered, keeping quiet to herself as (Y/N) looked down at Wednesday for a moment, "I'm sorry-- If I did anything wrong to you or anything like that--" (Y/N) muttered an apology, "If that's why you're ignoring me." (Y/N) finished looking at Wednesday.

That's when Enid woke up with a loud gasp which made (Y/N) yelp slightly as she dropped the photo on the ground in fright as she bent down to grab the papers making her grunt harshly gritting her teeth which made Wednesday notice. "Sorry--" (Y/N) apologized grabbing the photo as she looked at Wednesday, handing them to her as Enid looked at (Y/N) with wide eyes, "Are you real?" She asked in a shaky tone as (Y/N) nodded her head with a puzzled look, looking down at Wednesday, "Imma just make my way to class-- Cya there." (Y/N) waved off leaving Enid on the ground like a lost puppy.

"And she forgot her hoodie." Wednesday sighed as her eyes flickered at the (F/C) hoodie that sat on her desk as she looked down at Enid. "Enid, get up now. We have to go to class." Wednesday began as she packed up her stuff, walking out of there as Enid's eye's looked at the pictures making her scramble to her feet, dashing out of there.

(Y/N)'s stepmother, Marilyn Thornhill, would distinctively talk in the background as the two girl's from earlier sat next to each other. (Y/N) looked down to grab her book from her bag as three large claw marks were seen near her nape from Wednesday which made her notice as (Y/N) grunted softly in pain, retrieving her book.

(Y/N) looked down at Wednesday hesitantly for a moment, "Bianca and I had a duel in fencing yesterday, eheh." (Y/N) lied accordingly as she flipped a few pages in her book which made Wednesday grow curious. (Y/N) was too busy sketching to even care about what the class was bickering about.

(Y/N) then looked down at her book, her eyes suppressing emptiness as she looked at Wednesday. "You're not gonna volunteer?" (Y/N) stifled a small chuckle, "Aren't you pumped about the disco balls and spiked punch?" (Y/N) questioned jokingly nudging Wednesday with a small yet pained smile. "There's even a DJ. MC Blood Suckaz." (Y/N) acknowledged, her eyes never leaving the paper.

"I'd rather stick needles in my eyes," Wednesday muttered to the girl as she would chuckle dryly, using her powers to make a black dahlia spring out. (Y/N) would finally look at

Wednesday with a small and warm smile as she offered her it. Wednesday looked taken aback as she looked at (Y/N), creasing her eyebrows. "I'll probably do that anyways." She looked away as she packed up her stuff leaving which made (Y/N) look at the figure disappearing in the distance, she then looked at the dahlia as it disappeared in her hands, crumbling softly into nothing but ash.

(Y/N) had the faintest idea to go to her art studio from earlier as she continued to draw and sketch a few pictures. She couldn't help it since it kept appearing in her dreams, and couldn't get over it.

(Y/N) eventually looked at the canvas she drew hesitantly, revealing the monster as she just shrugged it off, proceeding to grab her belongings and walk out of there for her next class. Little did (Y/N) know, a certain Black-haired girl was watching her in the distance as she walked out of there.

"We need to do this." Wednesday whispered to Thing, "(Y/N) didn't get those scratches from fencing." She then acknowledged, "She's hiding something." She muttered as she walked to her art studio, opened up the door, and slipped inside.

Wednesday looked around anxiously as she turned on the light looking at the canvases full of horrific creatures. "I suppose every artist needs a muse." The girl muttered to herself. Wednesday grabbed a few papers and examined them which had spiral patterns on them aswell as the creature as her eyes drifted to a blood-stained hand towel.

"(Y/N), you just became much more interesting." Wednesday muttered as she examined the art pieces as began folding them up, flipping them in her blazer as she turned off the light and walked outside making sure to close the door behind her as she walked through the foggy forest as a voice called behind her, "Wednesday." The voice belonged to (Y/N).

"(Y/N)," Wednesday turned to face (Y/N), "Hello." Wednesday began as she creased her eyebrows at (Y/N) which made (Y/N) grow curious at her, "What are you doing?" (Y/N) questioned, "Nothing." Wednesday remarked as (Y/N) looked at her with a skeptical look, "I just saw you come out this way." Wednesday continued, "What is this place?" questioned Wednesday, "Oh-- It's kind of my private art studio." (Y/N) nodded, digging her hands into her pockets.

"I cleared it out, and fixed it up, so Principal Weems let me use it." (Y/N) nodded, "How very entrepreneurial. I would love to see inside." Wednesday acknowledged which made (Y/N)'s eyes widen, "Why don't you give me a tour." Wednesday began as (Y/N) looked down at Wednesday for a moment before shaking her head, "Not right now-- It's a total mess--" (Y/N) sighed. "I shadowed a crime scene photographer last summer." She began, "I'm not easily fazed." Wednesday interpretation.

"Maybe another time." (Y/N) began with a small shrug, "Anyways-- Why were you looking for me?" (Y/N) questioned, "I wanted to go over Miss Thornhill's homework assignment." Wednesday began, her hands clasped over each other which made (Y/N) much more curious, "She didn't give us homework--" (Y/N) remarked, "Remember?" (Y/N) began as Wednesday looked down for a moment, "Why are you really out here?--" (Y/N) questioned her arms falling to her side.

"Is this about a certain dance that makes you want to poke needles into your eyes, perhaps?" (Y/N) chuckled wryly, her warm smile coming back onto her face as she looked down at Wednesday for a moment. "I'm all ears." (Y/N) smiled as she placed both of her hands onto her hips swinging them side-to-side slightly.

"Are you really going to make me ask?" Wednesday began, "Absolutely." (Y/N) smiled jokingly, as Wednesday would inhale wearily, "Would you..." She asked with a shaky breath, "Would--" She stammered, "Would you possibly consider going to the Rave'N dance with a certain..." She paused, "Would " She paused as (Y/N)'s cheeky expression faltered into a rather shocked one, realizing that she wasn't joking.

"Would you go to the dance with me?" She finally got the courage to ask as (Y/N) stood there with wide eyes, "Woah, Wednesday--" (Y/N) stammered, unsure of what to say.

"I thought you were going to go on about Xavier or even Tyler--"

"I wasn't really expecting that--" (Y/N) fidgeted with her hands which made Wednesday look at her with a hint of sadness in her eyes.

"I mean-- Yeah-- Yes-- Of course--" (Y/N) reassured, "I mean-- Yes, Wednesday. I'd love to go to the Rave'N dance with you." (Y/N) smiled, "I thought you'd never ask." (Y/N) sighed before shrugging, "Neither did I." she turned on her heel away from (Y/N) and (Y/N) looked at her as she disappeared, running off which intentionally made her shrug.

Enid would squeal happily, "Oh My God! Wednesday Addams is going to the Rave'N!" She squealed in delight, "With the one and only, (Y/N) (L/N)?!" She squealed loudly with every breath she took, "My whole world is tilted!" She smiled excitedly as Wednesday stood there in shock at her actions.

"Why are you so excited?" Wednesday questioned in her dismal tone as Enid paused for a moment and looked at her for a moment, "Well, (Y/N) hasn't really been at the Rave'N ball before, last year she was supposed to go with Bianca Barclay, but had to go work. Bummer." Enid sighed, and then looked at Wednesday, her smile forming back.

"Do you know what you need?" Enid questioned, "A bullet to the head?" Wednesday replied sarcastically. "A dress!" Enid smiled, "I already have one." Wednesday determined, "Not the one you showed up in!" Enid remembered, "That thing was a fashion emergency, not even lighting could resuscitate." She began and then looked at Thing, "Thing back me up here." she looked as Wednesday looked at him as he did a thumbs up which made Wednesday glare at him.

"You need something that screams, 'First Date. Stand back bitches! I have arrived!'" She smiled eagerly, "And I know just the place!" She smiled happily.

Enid and Wednesday stopped near a dress shop, but Wednesday refused to go there so she decided to go to the local Police station, stopping near her therapist and having a conversation with her.

Wednesday had given Sheriff Galpin a drawing that belonged to (Y/N) as it had a drawing of the monster, but as the two of them, the man requested Wednesday to give hard concrete evidence on the mysterious person behind the case as Wednesday left with the paper in her hand.

Wednesday walked near the Weathervane where (Y/N) supposedly was as Tyler had just finished coming off shift. "Don't want to ask what trouble you're in now." Tyler began as he walked up to Wednesday, "Nothing I can't handle." Wednesday replied. "Your father's in particularly frustrating form today. Avoid." Wednesday warned as Tyler looked down at her, raising his eyebrows.

"Well, Welcome to my world." He sighed, "You guys have the Rave'N this weekend, right?" Tyler questioned making Wednesday look down with a dark look, "It was all the buzz at the Weathervane today." Tyler continued, "I must be the only one not obsessed with this stupid dance." Wednesday scoffed accordingly.

"So, you're not going?" Tyler questioned, "Actually, I was forced to ask someone as an act of self-preservation." She began, looking up at Tyler's soft hazel eyes. "Sure, that happens, I guess." Tyler shrugged, looking down at her. "So, who is it?" Questioned Tyler, Wednesday paused for a moment looking down at the ground, before making eye contact with Tyler. "(Y/N)." She uttered as she looked at him as his look changed into sadness slightly as he looked down at the ground.

"Got it." He muttered in sadness, "Hope you two have fun." He began as he brushed passed her as she turned around, "I'm not sure why you're upset." She began, "That's kind of the problem." Tyler uttered, "I mean, call me crazy, Wednesday, but you keep giving me these signals." Tyler proclaimed, his voice lacing in sadness. "It's not my fault I can't interpret your emotional Morse code." Wednesday acknowledged.

"Then let me spell it out." Tyler shrugged angrily, "I thought we liked each other." Tyler began as Wednesday looked at him, unsure of what to do. "But then you pull something like this, and I have no idea where I stand." Tyler sighed, "Am I in the 'More-than-friend zone' or just a pawn in the game you're playing?" He questioned as Wednesday looked down slightly, "I'm just dealing with a lot right now." Wednesday shuddered, "I need to prioritize." She looked up at Tyler as he just looked at her for a moment, "Thanks for clearing that up." He began, "I guess, give me a call if I ever move up your to-do list." He insisted before leaving Wednesday there.

Wednesday eventually went back to the school and to the club where she left the collage of photos she had of those people, along with those sketchers.

Eugene figured out where the spiral of the monster emerged from as Wednesday decided to retrieve a few things in (Y/N)'s art studio. 'Hard Evidence' she called it. Wednesday used a paintbrush to pick up the blood-stained towel and a few others things from the bin as the door opened to (Y/N) as she was humming to herself until she paused when she saw Wednesday.

"Wednesday? W-what are you doing--" (Y/N) asked in a weary voice as she darted her eyes around the room Wednesday looked at her and then questioned, "How do you know what the monster looks like?" She questioned as (Y/N) eyes widened, "Or are these just self-portraits." Wednesday raised an eyebrow that made (Y/N) scoff in disbelief at her, sadness wavered in her voice, "What?-- Do you think it's me?-- I literally saved your life--" (Y/N) shook her head looking down at Wednesday.

"So did the monster. Or was that you the night Rowan was killed?" Wednesday interpretated with a question, looking at (Y/N) as her eye's pricked with tears, "You are so out of line right now-- I--" (Y/N) was cut off by Wednesday, "I'm trying to uncover the truth." Wednesday interpreted. "And your art seems to have a recurring motif." Wednesday began as she gripped her bag, (Y/N) looked at her with sad eyes, "Yeah." She muttered warily, "This-- This monster--" She pointed at one of the canvases, "This monster has been haunting me for the past few weeks." She began.

"I try to block it out-- But I can't..." (Y/N) sighed rubbing her temples with her non-mechanical hand, "So I just, come in here and paint it." she shrugged looking down at Wednesday with tired eyes, "When I was painting this one, claws reached out and took a swipe at me." (Y/N) mumbled loud enough for Wednesday to hear, "That's how I got those scratches." (Y/N) began.

"I thought you were able to control your ability." Wednesday began as (Y/N) shook her head, "Not when it comes to this thing." (Y/N) muttered, looking at the painting. "Maybe it's your guilty conscience," Wednesday remarked as (Y/N) looked down at Wednesday with a look of disbelief before saying, "I told you, I'm not the monster, okay?" She began, as she looked down at Wednesday raising her voice slightly, "If you didn't hear correctly from your roommate Enid-- I'm a cyborg." (Y/N) looked down at Wednesday with a stern look, crossing her arms.

That's when Wednesday dug into her bag and grabbed a sketch of the monster which made (Y/N) eyes widen. "You just happen to draw pictures of it, down to the location of its lair in the woods?" She questioned, as (Y/N) looked at her monstrous art pieces, "Those are some pretty vivid dreams." Wednesday spoke sarcastically as (Y/N) creased her eyebrows, no longer making eye contact with the pig-tailed-haired girl.

"You were in here." (Y/N) looked down in disbelief, "Before, when I caught you outside." (Y/N) looked down in disbelief as tears threatened to spill down her eyes. She just looked down shaking her head, "That's the only reason you asked me to the Rave'N?" (Y/N) questioned, furious now as her arms fell to the side.

A few strands of tears would escape (Y/N) eyes as she continued, making Wednesday look down, "To try cover-up?" (Y/N) scoffed in disbelief, "Is this what you think of me now?" (Y/N) shook her head.

"It's not like that, (Y/N)--" Wednesday tried to utter but (Y/N) just looked away from her with a pained expression.

"A monster. Wow." (Y/N) interpretated, and down at Wednesday. "That's-- That's Sick, Wednesday--" (Y/N) looked down at Wednesday, her arms shaking, "It's nothing personal--" Wednesday looked up, making eye contact with (Y/N).

"No, it never is with you, isn't it?" (Y/N) stammered as she wiped her tears using her non-mechanical hand as more intended to slide out, "I mean-- do you even care about anyone or anything at all, Wednesday?" (Y/N) glared down, gritting her teeth, internally telling herself not to cry, which of course failed.

Wednesday looked down for a moment, thinking to herself as (Y/N) looked at her teary-eyed, she then looked down and pointed at the door, "Just-- Just get out--" She motioned as the two locked eyes, Wednesday finally realizing her actions as she walked out of there as her eyes glossed with a thin layer of salt-water tears as she vowed to herself to not cry.

Wednesday slammed the door making (Y/N) look at Wednesday as she then broke out into tears.

Wednesday then stormed into the Police Station, intending to walk onto Sheriff Galpin who was on an important phone call as Wednesday came in.

Wednesday stopped in front of him as she slammed the items found in (Y/N) art studio making the sheriff look at her with a weirded-out expression. "That's the claw of the monster," She pointed out, "And that's the dried blood sample from a potential suspect." She looked down at the things she had stolen from (Y/N) earlier.

"She used it to dab scratches on her neck." Wednesday began as the sheriff examined it, "Run the DNA test and see if they match." She spoke, determined as she looked down at the objects laid out in front of her. "I'm sorry, do I work for you?" The sheriff exclaimed as he looked up at her, "You asked for concrete evidence. That's it." Wednesday acknowledged.

"Where'd you get this?" The sheriff questioned, grabbing a hold of the plastic-covered claw in his hand, "And who's the suspect?" He questioned again. "Run the test first, and then I'll explain everything." She looked at him, "I'm not playing games, Addams." He pointed at her with a serious look as she looked down at him with the same look. "Neither am I, Sheriff." She interjected as the man kept quiet as she pressed the button, "Bernice, bring me a DNA authorization form, please." The sheriff began.

Wednesday sent the sheriff a small smirk of her own as he did also.

Wednesday walked up to Eugene as he sat there next to (Y/N) as she was talking to him. Wednesday stopped in front of the two as (Y/N) looked between them, "Sorry. I'll go." (Y/N) sent Wednesday a small-down cast stare as she walked out of there, putting her hands in her pocket as she disappeared from view.

"I'm supposing (Y/N) isn't feeling well, since well-- You did kind of mean--" Eugene tried to make out as Wednesday looked down at him, glaring, "Finish that sentence and it won't be (Y/N) in that state." Wednesday began as Eugene sighed, "Sorry-- She was just talking to me about the two of you being on bad terms right now." He sighed once more, "I also feel bad for her, because, well. I'm not very eager to say this but I kind of feel her pain." He looked at Wednesday.

"How so?" Wednesday questioned, "You see, this would've been (Y/N)'s first prom," He acknowledged, "But now she's not going so--" He began with a shrug as Wednesday looked where (Y/N) was standing as she was painting a raven mural. "But anyways," He began, "It's pretty much about Enid too. I asked her if she got my honey, and she said no," The boy looked down in sadness.

Wednesday then got the idea that since the two didn't have any partners for the Rave'N dance, the two talked to one another about the Rave'N as they planned to venture into the mysterious cave and try to identify the monster. "Whoever it may be." She whispered as she looked into the distance, seemingly disheartened as she saw both (Y/N) and Bianca talk to one another, as Eugene and Wednesday left.

"So... I heard you might be free tomorrow night after all." Bianca smiled as she walked up to (Y/N) and stepped down with a humble smile, "Yeah." (Y/N) chuckled lightly, looking down into Bianca's baby blue eyes as she sent her a warm smile of her own. "Would you-- Perhaps want to take me to the dance?" She questioned as (Y/N)'s ears perked up. "Yes-- of course." (Y/N) smiled, but then remembered, "As friends-- of course." (Y/N) looked down rubbing her neck as Bianca looked down with a sad smile, "Yes, Of course." She smiled as (Y/N) nodded, her wide smile coming back.

(Y/N) wasn't very fond of white clothing, so she decided to wear a black tuxedo, her hair in a (H/S), and dusted herself off and looked at herself one last time in the mirror before sighing, that's when a repetitive knock came at the door as (Y/N) assume it was Bianca but opened it to see the one and only, Enid Sinclair.

"Hey, (Y/N)!" Enid smiled widely as she looked at (Y/N), examining her. "You look so, SO GOOD!" She smiled widely as she came forward making (Y/N) step back. "Aren't you excited to take Wednesday?" She questioned whole-heartedly as (Y/N) looked down at her stunned for a moment, as she shook her head slightly.

"I'm not taking Wednesday." (Y/N) sighed, looking at Enid with a sad look, before smiling lightly, "But I am taking Bianca." She began as Enid's face scrunched up slightly and Enid looked at her seriously for a moment, "Are you serious?-- With her?--" Enid's eyes widen as (Y/N) looked behind her, "Speak of the siren." (Y/N) smiled as she looked behind Enid, which was Bianca leaning on the door eyeing (Y/N) up and down. (Y/N) sent her a small smile as she chuckled which made Enid look behind her.

"Sorry-- I'll get going. My date is probably waiting for me." She began and walked out of the room as (Y/N) raised an eyebrow, before shrugging. "Alright then, we'll see you there." (Y/N) waved off as Enid was already gone in a dash. (Y/N) held her arm out for Bianca and she happily accepted. "You look good, Bianca." Pluto complimented as Bianca smiled at her, "You do as well, (Y/N)." The two smiled as they walked to the Rave'N dance, they were greeted and introduced by Miss Thornhill and the Principal.

A few others looked at (Y/N) since she was the only one dressed in black as Bianca and (Y/N) smiled at each other and joked around with one another.

(Y/N) and Bianca were having the time of their lives as they danced around the dance floor listening to the DJ boost up loud and impressive music.

(Y/N) then sat down on the table with a yeti-tini as she was gulping a lot of them as she was already on her tenth glass. "Does your mood have to do with a certain pig-tailed goth girl?" She questioned as (Y/N) looked at her with a small smile, "She's not here. We are." Bianca reassured as she rubbed (Y/N) back reassuringly. (Y/N) looked at her with a smile.

"You're right." (Y/N) remarked, "I'm Sorry. Let's go have fun." (Y/N) smiled at her apologetically as she offered her hand to Bianca she happily accepted as the two went on the dancefloor. "Yo, check it out." Ajax muttered behind (Y/N) as (Y/N) looked to where the whole school was looking, "Wednesday totally busted out of her cocoon." Ajax began as he looked at (Y/N), "Ayo my man-- You're matching with Wednesday." Ajax pointed out as (Y/N) looked at Wednesday with wide eyes.

The people then looked between (Y/N) and Wednesday as (Y/N) just shook her head and grabbed onto Bianca's hand as they danced to the music, as Wednesday couldn't help but look at the two having fun in the distance as she held onto two glasses of yeti-tini's as (Y/N) noticed in the distance as she walked to Wednesday accordingly.

"I can't believe you bought him." (Y/N) muttered glancing at Tyler, "I should say the same." Wednesday muttered to herself, but then looked at (Y/N). "Why are you bringing this up?" Wednesday questioned, looking into (Y/N)'s mixed eyes. "As if this dance wasn't tedious enough." (Y/N) was taken aback and disheartened as she looked at Wednesday, "Because you don't know what he did to me." (Y/N) sighed looking at her dark eyes compared to (Y/N)'s as her eyebrows creased slightly.

Wednesday then glanced at her date and then at (Y/N), "Enlighten me." She gazed as (Y/N) as she sighed warily.

(Y/N) and Bianca were dancing to Goo Goo Muck as (Y/N) was dancing ironically as she saw in the distance that Wednesday as was dancing to it ironically aswell as (Y/N) followed Wednesday's dance move with a slight smirk of her own as Wednesday noticed in the distance, her's eyes widening.

Tyler and Bianca stood there in shock as (Y/N) and Wednesday looked at each other with a small smirk of their own as (Y/N) and Wednesday ironically got close together and followed each other's footsteps that's when (Y/N) looked around for Wednesday as she tapped her shoulder as she sent (Y/N) a small smirk as the two danced together making people around them notice along with the Principal.

That's when the song finally ended as (Y/N) laughed whole-heartedly as she swung her arm on Wednesday's shoulder, "That was so awesome." (Y/N) cheered looking at Wednesday for a moment, her eyes widening as she stepped back. "Sorry- I wasn't sure if I was allowed to--" (Y/N) quickly apologized bowing her head as her eyes widened, making Wednesday's ones soften slightly.

"I should be the one apologizing." Wednesday looked down as (Y/N) looked down at her with a small smile as the song faded into Earth Angel, "This is to all you lovers out there." The DJ bashfully smiled.

(Y/N) and Wednesday looked at each other for a moment, "Would you like to dance?" (Y/N) questioned with a small smile, offering her left hand as Wednesday looked between Tyler and Bianca, and then at (Y/N) for a moment before smiling slightly.

"Of course." Wednesday smiled, accepting her hand as the two walked into the middle of the dancefloor as (Y/N) and Wednesday swayed softly to the rhythm, that is when Enid came to the two with a smug look on her face as she elegantly made (Y/N) place her hands on her hips and also Wednesday's as (Y/N) looked down at Wednesday with wide eyes for a moment, Wednesday did aswell.

(Y/N) looked down at her with a small smile before shrugging as she placed her head on her shoulder as the two danced close to one another, a look of jealousy coming over Tyler's and Bianca's whilst Wednesday and (Y/N) danced slowly to the music.

The music continued to play as Wednesday twirled around, her hand in (Y/N)'s until all of a sudden a few specks of red substance dropped on (Y/N)'s shoulder making (Y/N) stop for a second along with Wednesday as the two looked at each other for a moment as (Y/N) looked up at the pipes as they began to gurgle softly as more red substance would come down.

Wednesday then looked at it with a wide smile on her face as (Y/N)'s eyes widen as more came down, the music never stopping, that is until the students were eventually covered in it as they all looked at each other for a moment until they eventually screamed running out of there in terror as (Y/N) looked up aswell and then at Wednesday with a smile of her own.

People would then clamor into one another, desperate to get out of there as (Y/N) and Wednesday looked at each other, Wednesday would then use her index finger to lick the red substance off as she looked at it in disbelief, "They couldn't even spring for real pigs' blood." She began out loud, making (Y/N) chuckle slightly as the music was cut off due to the DJ making it off.

Wednesday turned around from (Y/N), mumbling, "It's only paint." Wednesday scoffed in disbelief as Pluto would then use her telekinetic powers to make the music play again Wednesday turned around to face (Y/N), "At least we can spend the night together, and maybe repair our friendship."

(Y/N) offered her hand as the two then danced together softly for what seemed like a few minutes with soft smiles implanted on their faces until the song eventually ended whilst the red pain rained down on them.

Tyler then came into view as he was trying to spike an argument with (Y/N) although the two's conversation was inaudible as Wednesday was knocked into Tyler having a chaotic vision of Eugene in danger as because one of the many students had tripped Wednesday over as (Y/N) caught her in her arms as she held onto her before she made an impact on the ground.

"Be careful next time." (Y/N) scolded, Wednesday looked at her for a moment as Miss Thornhill came into view,

"Wednesday! Are you okay?" The woman questioned, "Eugene is in the woods. He's in danger." Wednesday began as she immediately dashed out of there, (Y/N) looked at her with wide eyes as she disappeared making (Y/N) look around anxiously.

(Y/N) eventually apologized to Bianca for leaving her there at the prom, which Bianca understood, and eventually went with Xavier until they had a small argument of some sort, which Pluto nodded.

After that, (Y/N) decided to walk back to her dorm as she was drenched in red paint as she went for a long and relaxing shower, trying to get the paint off her, which she eventually did as (Y/N) decided to crash in bed after that, thinking about Wednesday with a small smile on her face before drifting off to sleep.

Chapter Five, You Reap What You Woe.

3RD PERSON'S POINT OF VIEW.

Wednesday would stand at the Quad, looking at the police file which showed her father on it, along with (Y/N)'s as they had their own separate photo, smirking at the camera as he resembled (Y/N) which made Wednesday look at the following picture examining the man's features as she looked up to where (Y/N) was standing, where the incident happened beyond 30 years ago.

Wednesday was in a daze as she didn't notice the (H/C) haired girl floating down towards her, "Hello, Wednesday." She began with a small smile making Wednesday blink slightly, "Hello." Wednesday began as she looked at (Y/N) uncomfortably which made (Y/N) realize, "Oh-- Sorry-- I thought we were on good terms again because of last night." (Y/N) shrugged as she looked down at the ground.

"Other than that, it *is* Parents' Weekend." (Y/N) remarked, "Are your parents gonna come?" (Y/N) asked as Wednesday nodded her head in disbelief, "Yeah. Sadly." The girl began making (Y/N) chuckle, "Luckily for me, my stepmother will greet the parents and be busy all day." (Y/N) negotiated looking around the Quad, "Although, on the positive side, there is free food." (Y/N) smiled as Wednesday nodded.

"I'll be hanging out in my dormitory if you need anything." (Y/N) smiled down at Wednesday, "Or perhaps at my art studio, it depends." (Y/N) began looking down at Wednesday with a small-sad smile, "You do realize that you could've just asked-- I would've cleaned it up a little bit--" (Y/N) sighed which made Wednesday look up at her with a slight glint of happiness, "Oh." She fumbled, "I'm sorry for the intrusion." She paused looking down, "And my behavior." She apologized as (Y/N) looked down at her with wide eyes, they soon softened, "It's quite alright." (Y/N) began as she looked at the door opening too many parents.

"I best be off now, take care, Wednesday." (Y/N) waved off leaving Wednesday there with a small smile, before slapping herself to control herself.

(Y/N) and Bianca stood next to each other as they stared down at the many people reuniting with their families,

"Not sure how much more of this family togetherness I can take." (Y/N) chuckled jokingly looking at Bianca and then at the reunited people. "Tell me about it." Bianca stifled a laugh looking at (Y/N) for a moment, "I'm guessing Miss Thornhill is busy with the guests?" Bianca began as (Y/N) nodded for a moment, "But it doesn't bother me." (Y/N) shrugged, "How about you?" Questioned (Y/N).

"Gabrielle hasn't shown her face since I started here." Bianca sighed sadly looking down at (Y/N) as (Y/N) placed a comforting hand on her shoulder, "Probably sunning herself in the Seychelles." Bianca shrugged until the familiar voice came into view.

"My darling daughter." A woman's voice began as (Y/N) and Bianca turned to face the woman which made (Y/N) shocked as the woman eyed (Y/N) down in disgust, and then at Bianca with a wide phony smile. "I made it." She remarked as she looked down at (Y/N) for a moment, "Are you... still with her?" She questioned as her face scrunched up in disbelief and disgust, trying to hide it, which made (Y/N) just look down at Bianca.

"I'll let you deal with her." (Y/N) sighed, walking away leaving Bianca to face her mother.

(Y/N) overheard the conversation coming from Larissa Weems as she was going on about Eugene in the hospital, so (Y/N) decided to head over there for a bit in her black car.

Once (Y/N) entered the room, it didn't look like anyone was there to see him, so she decided to sit next to him. "Hello there, Eugene. If you can hear me." (Y/N) began with a shaky sigh, "I bought honey for you--" (Y/N) began as she placed it on the nightstand next to him.

"I didn't know that you were in the hospital, my dear friend." (Y/N) sighed as she sat next to him, "I've been thinking about Wednesday lately." She began with a faint-sad smile, "But I think that she doesn't like me as a friend, hm?" (Y/N) hummed sadly, "Not even more than that..." She fiddled with her fingers talking to the male in a coma. (Y/N) spent a few more minutes talking to Eugene until she eventually fell asleep by his side on the chair since she had nothing better to do.

Wednesday would then walk into the room and was escorted by a nurse inside as she was taken aback when she saw (Y/N) sleeping as she blinked, the door closing behind her. Wednesday walked to the nightstand as she placed down the jar of honey with a small sigh, grabbing a chair and sat next to (Y/N).

Wednesday whispered to Eugene softly, "I harvested at hive number three." She began as the monitor would beep softly. "The bees miss you, Eugene." Wednesday looked down at (Y/N) and then at Eugene, "We all do." She finished as (Y/N)'s eyes flickered open she looked at Wednesday for a moment as she fumbled slightly, using her sleeve to wipe off her saliva in a panic.

"How long was I asleep for--" (Y/N) grunted, using her arms to stretch as she looked at the pig-tailed girl as she just shook her head looking at Thing who hid behind the monitor the entire time making (Y/N)'s eyes widen. "Thanks for keeping an eye on him." Wednesday began as (Y/N) look like she had seen a ghost. "Any updates?" Wednesday asked as (Y/N) looked at Thing as her eyes pleaded at him for a moment until he shrugged making (Y/N) sigh in relief.

Wednesday noticed but didn't seem to care as her eyes were fixated on Eugene. "I should be the one in that bed," Wednesday muttered to herself as (Y/N) hesitantly put her hand on her back. "Wednesday, please don't say something like that." (Y/N) muttered, "But it's true." She replied, not even wanting to make eye contact with (Y/N).

That's when a woman tapped on (Y/N)'s and Wednesday's shoulders which made the two gasp lightly as they looked behind them seeing two women who seemed nice and warm. "Didn't mean to startle you, dear." One of the ladies smiled warmly, "You must be Wednesday." One of the ladies pointed to Wednesday as the other ladies looked at (Y/N).

"And you must be Eugene's newest friend, (Y/N)." The ladies smiled, "Eugene's moms, Sue and Janet." The ladies introduced themselves which made (Y/N) smile respectfully at the two, "The two of you were all he could talk about lately." Sue smiled warmly, "He was so happy that you, Wednesday, that you managed to join the Hummers." Janet smiled, "And also happy to make friends and step out of his comfort zone." Sue smiled.

"Eugene hasn't had the easiest time fitting into Nevermore." Janet sighed sadly, looking at her son who slept peacefully, "He was so excited to make real friends." Sue smiled at the two, "I never expected for him to be friends with such a lovely couple," Janet smiled widely as (Y/N) and Wednesday looked at each other for a moment, looking back at the two ladies with flustered expressions.

"I-- We bought him some honey." Wednesday nodded respectfully as (Y/N) side glanced at Wednesday with a small smile for a moment, as she was about to walk off until Janet notified, "Eugene loves those dang bees like they're his kids." Janet smiled, "His fuzzy-buzzy babies" The woman began as her partner flinched slightly in sadness.

(Y/N) noticed as she placed her hand on Wednesday's shoulder, "We should head out and give you two some space." (Y/N) smiled warmly as the women nodded sadly as Wednesday and (Y/N) walked out of there, dropping her hand to the side as Wednesday looked down in sadness.

"Hey-- Hey. It's not your fault." (Y/N) rubbed her back as the two walked out of the hospital.

(Y/N) and Wednesday walked next to each other as the two stood in front of the decaying statue of Joesph Crackstone. "He's a dick." (Y/N) acknowledged, "I'm guessing Thing did this." (Y/N) remarked trying to cheer up the black-haired girl as Wednesday nodded with a small smirk of her own.

"Anyways," (Y/N) turned to face Wednesday, "I forgot to ask, did you find anything about our father's case?" (Y/N) questioned, "Yeah." Wednesday began, her smile fading, "They were murderers." Wednesday began as she looked up at (Y/N), "Anyways, I believe my mother is surprisingly worried about my outburst from earlier." Wednesday looked down with a small sigh as (Y/N)'s eyes flickered to her mother as she walked to the cemetery, making (Y/N) look at Wednesday.

"I'm guessing this is Goodbye, at least for now." (Y/N) smiled, clasping her hands behind her as Wednesday looked at (Y/N) with a small nod, "Alright then, I'll be at school if anything." (Y/N) smiled with a wave, walking backwards as she turned around flying back to her 2004 ford, Wednesday looked at her flying until she was out of view.

Wednesday then looked at her mother who walked with a red-velvet colored rose, as she felt skeptical and followed her. The woman stood in front of a headstone as she ripped the petals of its stem as she looked down, her eyes filled with fury and tears, throwing the stem on top. Wednesday opened the gate to the cemetery as she walked to the headstone her mother stood in front of as it showed, 'Garret Gates' engraved into it.

They were at the Academy as Wednesday's mother commented, holding onto a plate of food, "Mmm, I am famished." She commented, "You're not hungry, darling?" Her mother questioned, "My appetite eludes me, Mother." Wednesday paused, looking at her mother, "The same way the truth eludes you." She finished, brushing past her.

"We need to tell her." Gomez walked next to Morticia who saw her daughter go past her, flinching as she looked back at her husband, "She'll never believe us." She paused, looking in the distance as they saw a girl with (H/C) hair which was, of course, (Y/N) as their eyes widened making Morticia nearly faint which made Gomez place his hand on her shoulder. "Cara mia, don't be alarmed." He sighed lightly, examining the girl in the distance as she looked at Wednesday with a warm smile.

"You're right." The woman began, fixing her posture, "We must stay strong." She remained calm, her eyes still looking at the girl in the distance, "And hope that something more morbid comes along to distract her." She paused, "Which I believe is happening as we speak." She looked down at her husband with a smirk.

Xavier, Ajax, and (Y/N) sat next to each other as their plates were filled with food, (Y/N) and Xavier dug in as Ajax waved at Enid. (Y/N) stuffed her face as her eyes darted around the Quad for Wednesday until they eventually locked eyes with each other which made (Y/N) cough loudly, choking on her food as she used a napkin to wipe her face and then she gulp on her food down in one bite, waving at Wednesday slightly, accidentally wacking Ajax.

"Ow dude--" He complained which made (Y/N) place her hand on her scarred neck, embarrassed as she rubbed it. "Sorry-- Sorry..." (Y/N) apologized, looking back at Wednesday with a soft smile, until all of a sudden, the door opened up to reveal police officers which made (Y/N) crease her eyebrows.

"Can I ask what this is about, Sherrif?" The principal came forward as (Y/N) dropped her fork on her plate, skeptical making Xavier glance at her and then at the police officers. "What's happening Miss Thornhill?" Yoko asked as the woman shook her head, "I have no idea--" She looked ahead, as many people looked at the officers walking into the Quad.

"Gomez Addams." Sheriff Galpin's voice boomed aloud, making the poor man stand up as his family members looked at the police officers, horrified about what was going to happen. "Can I help you, Sheriff?" he asked, "You're under arrest for the murder of Garret Gates." The officer walked behind the man, putting his hands in handcuffs as his wife looked at him in terror, her eyes glossing with tears as (Y/N) lowered her fork and knife looking at Wednesday in the distance, her eyes widening.

The police officer kept talking to him as Pugsley's voice could be heard, disheartened in the distance, "Dad?" he stood up until the man was eventually dragged out of there. Wednesday looked at (Y/N), and then at her mother, her eyes were filled with a thin layer salt water.

(Y/N) looked at Wednesday for a moment before turning her head in a direction motioning for her to talk to her. Wednesday nodded, as (Y/N) left the table, Wednesday following her until they eventually were in front of the nightshade's entrance.

"Wednesday-- What happened?" (Y/N) asked, sad for the girl as Wednesday looked up at her with a small shrug. "I-- I'm not so sure." She uttered as (Y/N) looked down at the girl as immediately embraced her, as Wednesday stood there in shock, as she softened a little. "Investigate what the commotion, and maybe we'll talk about it." (Y/N) sighed, breaking the hug as Wednesday looked at her for a moment before nodding as (Y/N) and Wednesday walked back to their tables.

Wednesday sat in front of the glass pane waiting for her father to come as he was escorted by a security guard as he sat down with a heavy sigh, looking up at his daughter, seeing his noble friend, Thing crawl upon the desk that Wednesday sat in front of, placing his hand on the glass, Gomez doing also with a smile.

"My little Tormenta, how's your mother?" Gomez asked, "Devastated. She hates you in orange." Wednesday began, looking at him with a stern look. "I caught her laying a rose in a grave earlier today." Wednesday commented, "The headstone read, Garret Gates." Wednesday continued, "The very boy you've been arrested for murdering." Wednesday continued as Gomez looked down, pained.

"Care to explain?" She questioned with a serious look, "Garret was infatuated with your mother." The man sighed, shuffling uncomfortably, "And also (M/N)." He commented, looking at Wednesday with a dead-serious look, "(M/N)?" Wednesday questioned, "Yes." He muttered, "(M/N) (M/M/N) (L/N)." He sighed, looking down at the ground, "But that woman was taken with another man named (F/N)." He smiled, "I used to call him (F/N/N). Fun guy." He commented as Wednesday raised her eyebrows.

"I'm presuming his last name is (L/N)." She hummed looking at her father as he nodded, "So then that man decided to destine himself with your mother." He continued his story, "He mistook her kindness, for interest." The man began, "His infatuation turned into obsession, and started stalking her." Gomez looked up, remembering that night.

"Why didn't you call the police?" Wednesday questioned, "We tried." Gomez looked down with sadness, "But his family were the oldest and richest in Jericho." Gomez interjected, his voice still calm. "No one believed us." The man looked down for a moment. "Garret's father, an outcast-hating bigot, was furious that your mother and (M/N) had accused his only son."

"It all came to a head the night of the Rave'N dance."

"Your mother and I stepped out to catch our breath."

A young version of Morticia and Gomez would passionately kiss each other under the lit chandelier as the weather was cold and damp as it rained harshly, lightning scattering around the dark sky.

"And that's when I saw them."

A girl with (M/H/C) would run up the stairs, hand in hand with a boy around her age the two look like they had seen a ghost as the woman yelled, "Morticia!" The girl tripped on her own feet, making the boy next to her quickly pick her up as a boy ran up the stairs mere inches behind them until the two panted, standing next to the black-haired couple.

"And him."

"Addams!" The man yelled, looking at Gomez as the mixed-haired couple held onto each other in terror.

"He had broken into the school. His twisted love for your mother had made him insane."

"His eyes bore into me, brimming with murderous intent."

"Go. Get out of here. He won't hurt me." The black-haired woman ushered the three as (M/N) nodded, along with the other two as (F/N) quickly gripped onto Gomez's wrist as they ran out of there.

"Garret! No!" Morticia pleaded in the distance as he gripped the sword that was near him, chasing the three, "Garret! Stop!" The three ran up the stairs until they were eventually near a construction area since it was being renovated. Gomez swiftly grabbed onto a metal pole and began to strike Garret.

Gomez was eventually knocked onto the ground as he looked up in terror as the boy held a sword up in the air, beginning to strike him.

"My Life flashed before my eyes."

(F/N) interfered, making (M/N) yell out "No! (F/N)!"

"Until that man, saved my life."

The (F/H/C) haired man grabbed a metal object of his own as the two fought together, Gomez getting back on his feet, helping (F/N), as the two backed up a little, unsure of what to do to the man.

"Driven by jealousy and hate, Garret was unstoppable."

Garret plunged at (F/N), which he swiftly dodged, as Gomez grabbed onto the sword, making (F/N) kick him on the ground until he eventually managed to punch him making him stunned as he fell back, leaving Gomez to be thrown and tossed around until two eventually ended up on an unstable scaffold.

(F/N) groaned softly as blood trickled down from his head as (M/N) rushed to him with a horrified and worried expression as the two looked with wide eyes at their friend being tormented as Morticia begged for him to stop as she ran to where the couple sat looking in terror for Gomez.

Gomez strained against Garret as Morticia begged for him to stop, he was eventually pushed back forcefully near the sword, making (F/N)'s eyes widen along with (M/N)'s.

"When I saw the sword, my survival instinct kicked in."

Gomez clasped onto the sword that was next to him as he stood up tiredly, facing the sickened weirdo.

(F/N) watched in terror as the man quickly stormed up towards him, the metal object in his hand as he nearly struck Gomez, as (F/N) yelled "No!" his arm was stretched out in front of him as he used his telekinetic powers to make him freeze as Gomez plunged him with the sword as everyone's eyes widened.

"It was a terrible accident."

The man would stumble back light-headed, Gomez pulled the sword out of him which made him gasp until he eventually fell to his death. Gomez stood there in shock as (F/N) looked at his partner, (M/N), and then at his friend before walking forward as he placed his hand on his shoulder as a loud shriek would be heard.

Larissa Weems would then look up in horror to see the two boys standing there, as Gomez held onto the sword, the man next to him, a hand on his hip looking down at the lifeless body.

Wednesday would have her hands clasped onto each other, her blank expression forever and always the same, but couldn't help but think about (Y/N)'s father and think about the characteristics the both shared, along with her mother.

"Thank you for being honest with me." Wednesday thanked him, examining her father's features for a hint of lies.

"I'm sorry, I wasn't a better father." Gomez looked at her in sadness, his eyes beginning to brew with tears. "Could we please do without the over display of emotion?" Wednesday questioned, as her father stopped for a brief moment, "I know they make you feel uncomfortable."

The two talked to each other, Wednesday finally believing him until she eventually left.

"We need to talk." Wednesday began, walking into Sheriff Galpin's office with a stern look as he poured a cup of coffee.

"How the hell did you get in?" He questioned, Wednesday stood there at the door with a serious look, "Bernice? Bernice!" The man yelled through the window, as Wednesday walked into the room, "She may or may not have received a call that her tabby car, Swifty, is being held for ransom." She began, walking into the room.

"My father, and also (Y/N)'s did not kill Garret Gates."

"Well, I have signed his confession, and he identified the saber he used to do it." The man snorted, "(Y/N)'s father isn't alive, so mercy on her." He shook his head, taking a sip of his coffee cockily.

"Although, both of which I'm about the deliver to the District Attorney." He paused as Wednesday had a blank look, "Gomez-- I'm talking about." Wednesday realized and nodded, before sighing. "Don't you find the timing a tad bit convenient?" she walked forward to the man, "The Cornor kills himself out of remorse for a decades-old murder case, the very weekend that my father, your prime suspect deigns to return town." Wednesday began, her voice raising with each word she said.

"All I see is a guilty man who's finally going to pay for his crime." The man concluded, "And cuffing him myself, oh, that was the icing on the cake." The man negotiated smugly, which made the girl scowl internally, pissed off by the man's behavior and actions.

"How are you failing to see that someone is desperately trying to derail my investigation?" Wednesday questioned furiously. "I found the monster's cave, and I gave you the DNA evidence." She paused, "Did you even bother to test it?" She asked, "This may come as a shock, but the world doesn't revolve around you, Addams." She glared, grabbing the results from his drawer, and sliding them across the desk.

"Here. The DNA results." He began, "No match. Inconclusive." He remarked, "So you truly believe this is all some coincidence?" Wednesday questioned, "Whoever hurt Eugene, also hurt the Coronor." She remarked as the two bickered forwards and backwards until the two eventually gave up and then left, as the sheriff talked about Garret's family, on how they all passed on after his death.

On how his mother, *hung* herself.

His father, drank alcohol until he *overdosed*.

His sister was orphaned and sent overseas until eventually *drowning*.

(Y/N) would wander around the school her hands in her pocket as the autumn breeze whipped through her hair as her head hung low as she had her hands down in her pocket, her headphones blasting loud music.

Until she eventually bumped into a crying Enid.

"Oops-- Sorry--" (Y/N) apologized looking up to see Enid crying, "(Y/N)-- I--" Enid began, as a few tears rolled down her cheeks. "Ayo-- What's up--" (Y/N) ripped off her headphones and placed her two hands on her shoulders. "Enid-- what's wrong?" (Y/N) questioned as she was immediately embraced by the blonde-haired girl.

(Y/N)'s eyes immediately widened at the unexpected hug as she looked in the distance for a second to see her mother and her father standing there concerned, but then stopped once they saw (Y/N).

(Y/N) looked down at Enid for a moment before pulling away from the hug as (Y/N)'s shirt was drenched in tears and snot which made (Y/N) a tad bit taken apart, but did intentionally feel sorry for her friend. Wednesday saw in the distance as (Y/N) weakly smiled and waved at her before (Y/N) walked her back to her dorm as cleaned her up.

When (Y/N) was finished cleaning up Enid, Enid couldn't help but smile down at (Y/N). "Thank you for being a nice friend." She thanked with a sad smile as (Y/N) was cut off, "No pro--" Wednesday walked into the room, before grabbing onto (Y/N)'s hand as was pulled out leaving Enid there as (Y/N) waved at the girl, "Uh Bye-- I guess?--" (Y/N) began as the door closed behind her.

"Wednesday-- What's the big idea?--" (Y/N) questioned, her eyebrows creased as Wednesday kept quiet until they eventually reached the statue of the poet himself.

"You'll see." Wednesday sighed, snapping her fingers twice as she held onto (Y/N)'s hand and was eventually dragged downstairs, where a woman in a black dress that clung her body stood, as (Y/N) grew skeptical as the woman looked at a portrait of (M/N) and (F/N) as (Y/N) kept quiet. "Hello, Mother." Wednesday's voice echoed throughout the room as the two effortlessly walked down the stairs, the woman whipped her head behind as she saw the two.

"Hello, Wednesday." Her mother greeted, her eyes darting to (Y/N), remembering she was that same girl earlier.

"And you are?" She questioned, as (Y/N) looked at Wednesday for a split second, "Mother, this is (Y/N)." She paused as her mother stepped close to her, "(Y/N) (L/N)." Morticia's eyes widened as she looked at the (H/C) haired girl. "As in, (F/N/N)'s Daughter?" The woman questioned, elegantly walking up to the girl as the girl stood behind Wednesday as she had a confused look, "(F/N)-- I mean." The woman examined the girl's admirable features which made her mildly uncomfortable.

The woman smiled softly at (Y/N), (Y/N) fidgeting her hands slightly as the woman looked down at her daughter who was embarrassed. "So, The two of you are nightshades?" The woman questioned, "Didn't take that long." She smiled at the two, "Actually, I rejected them." Wednesday acknowledged the woman and glanced at

(Y/N) as she shrugged, "I recall no memory of it." (Y/N) shrugged.

The woman then looked at Wednesday with a saddened look, "Why? Because I was a member?" She questioned, "I'll never live up to your legacy here," Wednesday stared down, "So why try?" Wednesday looked down for a moment. "I win the Poe Cup," Wednesday began, "You claim it four times." (Y/N) kept quiet as she shuffled backwards awkwardly.

"I join the fencing team, you captained it." Wednesday looked down.

"Why would you send me somewhere I could only exist in your shadow?" Wednesday questioned in disbelief as (Y/N)'s eyes darted down at the girl, placing a comforting hand on her shoulder. "It's not a competition, Wednesday." The woman remarked, "Everything is a competition mother," The girl looked down as (Y/N) took her hand back to her side, as the woman flinched.

"Should I go, Wednesday?" (Y/N) asked, her eyes flickering to her mother who stood there, eyeing the poor girl. "No." Wednesday uttered, "You must stay here, and hear the truth." Wednesday began, as (Y/N) stammered slightly, but knowingly obliged.

Her mother then continued, with a saddened looked, "We used to be so much more," she continued, "Our mission was to protect outcasts from harm and bigotry," She then paused, before saying, "In fact, the group was started by an ancestor of your's from Mexico." She looked at (Y/N) for a moment. "One of the first settlers in America." She smiled lightly which made (Y/N) mumble out, "Astoria," whilst Wednesday muttered aloud, "Goody."

The woman kept quiet as (Y/N) and Wednesday looked at each other for a moment, before talking. "We both saw their painting at Pilgrim world." (Y/N) nodded her head respectfully, looking at Wednesday, "Oh." Morticia mumbled, "How ironic since Astoria was the one that killed Crackstone." Her smile faded, eyeing the (H/C) haired girl, her smile seemingly forming back into something more... *sinister*.

(Y/N)'s eyes widened, her eyes flickering to Wednesday, pressing her lips into a thin line.

"The Nightshades were secret but deadly to his oppression."

"I *know* why you've come here, Wednesday." The woman acknowledged, "So go on, ask." She pleaded as (Y/N) and Wednesday looked at each other for a moment, before her daughter asked, stuttering lightly. "Father and her one, didn't kill Garret Gates, did he?" Wednesday asked, which made (Y/N) intrigued to what their conversation turned out in.

Morticia looked at the two, her eyes watering slightly as she kept quiet before whispering, "No."

Thunder would clap within its dark clouds as rain poured heavily on the three men fighting each other, which made (M/N)'s eyes and also a very young Morticia's widen in horror at what the two girls are witnessing.

"By the time I made it up the stairs,"

Morticia's mouth would quiver, her hands shaking as Lucielle tapped her shoulder in a panic, "We have to stop them!" (M/N) yelled, gaining Morticia's attention in fright, looking at the love of her life fight for his life.

"I found your father, and Owen fighting for their lives. It was terrifying."

"Garret, No!" (M/N) yelled in agony as Morticia's eyes widened in terror, petrified at the man who dared to lay a finger on her man, along with Morticia's.

(F/N) was eventually flung to the wall making him grunt in pain, as Gomez effortlessly pushed him against a pillar as his eye's widened, making Morticia and (M/N) look at him in terror, he spun around and chased after Gomez.

Once Gomez and Garret left, (M/N) immediately ran to her partner, tears prickling in her eyes. "(F/N)-- I--" She muttered, her tears sliding down her cheek as everything was inaudible, the two looked at each other as blood would pour from his head, as she placed her hand on his cheek. "My darling, my dear." (F/N) muttered, "Save him." (F/N) coughed out, placing his hand on hers as he caressed his thumb on her hand reasurringly.

(M/N) eyes flickered in the distance to see Morticia picking up the sword as she was near to being struck by the crazy man, his eyes bulging, his mouth foamed as (M/N) eyes widened, as fear, instantly turned into rage and fury as she raised her hand, using her telekinetic powers, "No!" and in a flash, he was still as Morticia accidentally plunged him with the sword.

Morticia would shudder, with fear, agony, and regret in her eyes, the sword in her hands as she pulled it out from him. (M/N) eyes widened into realization with horror as she looked at her hands in regret as they shook.

"I'm a monster," (M/N) cried to (F/N), tears falling down her eyes as (F/N) looked at her with wide eyes before planting a small kiss on her lips."You're not, my love." He sighed, as he looked up at Gomez who took the sword from Morticia. (F/N) stumbled lightly as he tried to stand up, "No-- My love! You mustn't move!" (M/N) pleaded as (F/N) looked down at her with a small smile. (M/N) went to stand up next to him holding onto his hand with a sad smile as the two let go.

"It's quite alright, I'll be fine." He reassured as the man walked to where Gomez stood. He was holding onto the sword as (F/N) limped over to him, placing his arm on his shoulder, and looking at the body that fell, and to Larissa Weems.

Gomez then immediately turned around and informed the two girls to leave as Morticia and Lucielle were too stunned to speak, but quickly obliged.

"Tish, (M/N), You both need to leave, right now." Gomez warned as his eye's widened, "Go to your room, and lock the door." He began, "The two of you, were never here." The man muttered as (F/N) limped towards Gomez, placing a hand on (M/N)'s shoulder, "You understand me?" Gomez began as (M/N) placed a hand on her shoulder, (M/N)'s eyes widened with tears, "Quick Tish-- We must go--" (M/N) ushered as Gomez quickly grabbed onto (M/N) forearm. "Look after her for me, for now." He begged as (M/N) nodded, "And here-- Take this--Put this back on the table." He gave the sword to (M/N) as her eyes widened at the sight of blood but quickly nodded. The two quickly left, making (F/N) and Gomez look at each other in sadness.

"Your father's took the blame, in order to protect both me and (M/N)." Morticia sighed, her eyes fumed with sadness,

"Your's aswell, (Y/N)." Morticia began as (Y/N)'s eyes widened at the story, the withheld information, everything.

The story that Wednesday's father had told was false, (Y/N)'s lunatic of a father, (F/N), never had any telekinetic powers beyond his reach.

(Y/N)'s hands twitched as (Y/N) immediately bowed her head in respect, fleeing up the stairs with a look of defeat plastered on her face as she excused herself. She didn't know much of her parents, since her childhood was basically being studied, experienced on, and much more.

Wednesday looked at the (H/C) haired figure who left in a dash that stood there in shock and in disbelief, looking back at her mother, continuing to have a long and extended conversation with her mother, and bonding momentarily, as the two black-haired females proceeded to dig up the corpse that belonged to Garret Gates himself.

(Y/N) was left alone up in her room as her vampire roommate, Yoko recently left to go hang out with Bianca or someone to her liking.

(Y/N)'s mind was clouded with the conversation, she couldn't help but hug her pillow and try to sleep it off, which of course failed.

Until she soon enough drifted off to sleep, having a nightmare, experiencing what she faced when she was younger.

In her nightmare, it showed her father in a science lab, the walls were painted white with a hint of gray, her father allowed her to step into the large testing chamber, its walls felt like enclosing her, her father sending her a downcast stare as he nodded to the woman that stood next to him as she shuddered in terror, holding onto her stuffed animal toy as she wore a hospital gown of some sort.

"Father?" The sweet voice that belonged to (Y/N) called out, her eyes tearing up as she heard a clanking noise, proceeding to look up in terror.

What seemed like not tens, but hundreds of circular saws came from the roof above which wade (Y/N) scream in terror, making her drop her stuffed (F/A).

"Let me out!" She banged on the metal door, the weapon slowly coming down.

"Please!" She begged, her father looked through the thick glass, grabbing the microphone that boomed through the chamber, he sternly looked down, "Use your telekinetic powers." He switched the microphone off as (Y/N) squirmed on the floor, her eyes now filled with tears as it was near her face, without thinking she quickly put her arm over her face, her father looking at the little girl in terror.

The girl's eyes widened as she felt utter pain pulse throughout her arm, as warm liquid came from it as the weapon wouldn't stop coming down, until it was eventually torn off, which made her scream in pain and agony.

The man soon called off the experiment, and she was taken to their underground ER for further notice, as he shook his head in disbelief, a scowl formed on his face.

(Y/N) was in surgery for what seemed like a few years, although it was a few months as her body was stiff, and her mind was blank. She was technically dead.

Until her father, proceeded to ingrain a small chip that he has been working on for years. He was unsure if it'll help, but it sure did. (Y/N) woke up a few days later, her father was skeptical about her sudden appearance as she had one (F/C) where the device was within her brain, along with her (E/C) which she was born with, the suspicion quickly fell, as she was gifted with remarkable powers.

Her father had recently given her a mechanical arm that intended to grow as she grew.

There were no major issues with it, it only hurt as it was bolted within her flesh, but she grew up enduring the pain that was caused, and as years went by, the time being 2015, being hated, bullied, and such, being called a Tiger by her mentality, she was eventually put into Nevermore Academy, where he met Marilyn Thornhill, fell in love, and eventually got married.

(Y/N) and Marilyn being (Y/N)'s stepmother, bonded quite well, having a mother-daughter relationship since (Y/N) couldn't really recall her mother when she was younger.

(Y/N) told Marilyn about her sad and sickening past, as her father eventually passed on a few monghx after.

(Y/N) was on edge about it for a moment since she was put in the care of her stepmother, which was the best that's ever happened to her. She spent her time at the Nevermore Academy after her father's death, not knowing much about her parents or their history.

And as the looked behind her step mother in her dream, the same monster came charging at (Y/N).

(Y/N) woke up with a panicked daze with a small gasp as she groaned at the sun rays hitting her eyes.

The girl swung her legs off the bed, as she eventually got herself out of bed.

With her technopathy powers, she proceeded to look at the time which was approximately 10 am. (Y/N) groaned as she sluggishly went for a nice warm shower, throwing on some comfortable clothes.

A rhythmic knock was heard at the door. (Y/N) walked toward it, and opening it she saw Bianca, the girl immediately swung her arms around (Y/N) making her dumbfound, "Bianca?" (Y/N) questioned tiredly as the girl who longed for (Y/N).

"Are you alright?" (Y/N) asked, shuffling uncomfortably as Bianca tore the hug away, holding onto her robotic hand, "Yeah, I'm fine." She sighed, looking down, "You don't have to lie to me, you know that?" (Y/N) creased her eyebrows looking at the girl, "Tell me, what's wrong?" (Y/N) questioned as Bianca looked into (Y/N)'s eyes. "I have to go back home," She paused for a moment, "With my mother." She sighed, uncomfortable at the sudden tension.

"Awe, so sudden?" (Y/N) questioned, "You've been a great friend to me though," (Y/N) looked down, "Same here, (Y/N)." The girl looked down for a moment, keeping quiet until she had a notification blare on her phone from her mother.

"I have to go now," The girl began, "I'll cya later now, Pluto." The girl waved off, leaving (Y/N) there in shock, as the girl closed the door. (Y/N)'s eyes flickered to her bag, as she floated toward it, grabbing it as she looked to the window.

(Y/N) hesitantly walked to the window, opening it as she stepped onto the roof, swinging her bag on her back, closing the window behind her as she flew down near the quad, landing elegantly, as she dusted the sleeves of her clothes as she walked to her car, as skidded off to Weathervane where she worked at.

(Y/N) came back from her part-time job several hours later, as she agreed to take over Tyler's shift since he went elsewhere, which she didn't mind or pay any attention to that.

(Y/N) groaned, popping her back as she pulled up to the car park. The sky was carved with dark scenery, hollered with dark blue specks as there were bags under her eyes, exhausted from over-working herself.

(Y/N) eventually turned off the engine and grabbed onto her bag as people could be heard in the distance, screaming (Y/N)'s eyebrows creased together as she got out of her car, locking it as she put her keys inside her pockets, running to where the commotion was.

As she could smell smoke in the distance as she walked to where the sound was heard, as fire sprawled from the ground, reading, 'Fire will rain.'

(Y/N) floated up reading it cautiously, making her eyes widen, as she looked up to see Wednesday and Principal Weems across the distance as they stood on a balcony from the Principal's office.

Chapter Six, Quid Pro Woe.

3RD PERSON'S POINT OF VIEW.

Enid and (Y/N) would walk together in the room, and Enid giggled beside Pluto as the two talked beside one another until the two stopped, noticing Wednesday on the ground.

"Sorry--" (Y/N) fumbled, "We didn't mean to interrupt your..." (Y/N) began as Enid stood beside her, "Uh, do I even wanna know?" The girl questioned, Enid flicking on the light beside her, making (Y/N) seemingly hesitant.

"I was reaching into the black maw to contact a relative." She walked over the candles, walking up the two, "You should do the same, (Y/N)." She informed making Enid looking between the two for a moment, quite skeptical "Feels very on-brand for you." Enid began, as she looked at the wood on the ground that resembled an Ouija board, as the word on the wood was engraved the word, Goody.

"You have a relative named Goody?" Enid questioned, looking at the ground as Wednesday nodded.

"She was one of the original outcasts," (Y/N) shrugged making Wednesday nod her head, "You know, (Y/N)?" Enid questioned, her eyes widening as the girl nodded, "Yup. Indeed." (Y/N) smiled, looking down at the girl, "Along with Astoria." Wednesday mumbled, "Astoria?" Enid questioned, "Yes. Astoria (L/N)." Wednesday's eyes flickered to Enid's for a moment, "(Y/N)'s Ancestor." The girl acknowledged (Y/N) and then nodded.

"I've been attempting to summon her, but she seems to be ignoring my entreaties." Wednesday sighed tiredly as (Y/N) patted her back comfortingly, "Oh!-- Have you tried using one of my scented candles?!" Enid asked giddily making (Y/N) chuckle slightly.

"The aroma of steak tartare is to die for." Enid giggled until they both heard paper flutter to the now-closed door making (Y/N) look at it curiously as she walked towards it, bending down to grab ahold of it, making the other two look at each other and notice as they slowly approached (Y/N).

"Maybe Goody answered you after all." (Y/N) overheard Enid mutter to Wednesday as (Y/N) read the paper, her eyebrows creasing at the ransom letter that was supposedly placed at the doorstep as Wednesday stood by her side and handed the girl the note.

"Well, I doubt that she communicates through magazine cutouts." Wednesday examined the paper that read, 'If you want answers, meet inside Crackstone's crypt. Midnight.' (Y/N) stood up and placed her hand on Wednesday's shoulder, "Maybe we shouldn't go to that old man's crypt--" (Y/N) shuddered at the thought as Wednesday gave (Y/N) a blank stare for a moment.

The three were apparently walking through the woods as fog hovered throughout the area, (Y/N) was a bit skeptical for Wednesday and Enid as (Y/N) kept a sharp eye on the two just in case anything happens...

The three approached the large crypt as Enid clung onto (Y/N)'s arm, fearful for the towering building as the three approached. (Y/N)'s (F/C) eye glowed in the dark not needing a flashlight, however, Enid on the other hand was trembling in fear as she heard a twig snap as she immediately pointed in that direction, jolting in fright as she accidentally clawed making the girl yelp.

"Sorry, (Y/N)!" The girl apologized in fear, her claws disappearing as she heard another twig snap as she immediately pounced on (Y/N), "I-- Hey--" (Y/N) stumbled backward at the sudden jump, landing on the ground with a harsh landing, as the girl desperately clung onto (Y/N), "Oh my God. I'm going to die!" Enid shrieked making (Y/N) shake her head as she crushed (Y/N) onto the ground.

Wednesday turned around, noticing the two close together, she sighed shaking her head at the sudden impact. "The both of you insisted on coming along." Wednesday stared down at the two, (Y/N)'s organs were being crushed by Enid, "Can-- You-- Get-- Off me now--" (Y/N) gasped as Enid looked at her, "Sorry!" The girl scrambled onto her feet, immediately helping the girl up.

(Y/N) sighed, thankful for Enid getting off of her. "I was fine on my own." She glared at (Y/N) bitterly for a second as Enid and (Y/N) looked at each other as the girl shrugged at Enid as they noticed Wednesday walk towards the door as (Y/N) and Enid came up behind the girl.

Wednesday used her flashlight to have a look at the statues that glared down at them, as they all panned their flashlights at the door that creaked open.

(Y/N) looked around, her eyes skimming off into the distance, having a strange feeling. Her strange and ethereal feeling was cut off by Enid's voice, "(Y/N)? Hello?" She waved her hand in front of (Y/N) with a concerned look, she snapped her fingers twice in front of her face making her flinch, "Oh-- Sorry-- What was that?" Enid questioned, "Remember? Wednesday?" She questioned as (Y/N) looked at her, raising her eyebrow.

"What about her?" The girl questioned, noticing that the girl had gone inside, "Didn't you bring her a present?" She questioned which made (Y/N) snap out of her daze, "Oh--

Oh." (Y/N) looked down, feeling around in her pockets, "Got it." Pluto acknowledged, as she pulled out a small box, and inside had a black ring with a skull on it, the inner ring having the word engraved Wednesday on it, as its eyes had small red rubies in it.

The two waited outside as (Y/N) thanked Enid for telling her a few days ago that it was her birthday in a few days, and hearing that, (Y/N) drove to the nearest city alone in her black car after her act of kindness of fulfilling Tyler's shift, proceeding to have enough time to get Wednesday a present, one she wouldn't have.

With the help of her inheriting her parents' mountain-like fortune and coming of age, she bought Wednesday a real ring, filled with real scarlet red rubies.

"Anyways, what'd you get for Wednesday?" Enid asked as (Y/N) grabbed out a small box as Enid looked at her with a wide smile, "Are you going to propose to her?!" She asked all giddily as (Y/N) looked at her with a blank and dumbfounded expression.

"What-- No--" (Y/N) cut her off, with a scoff "It's just a cool ring I came across," (Y/N) examined, flicking open the box, making Enid's smile quickly fade. "Well, It suits her." Enid shrugged, her smile forming back.

"Surprise!" The two overheard as Enid quickly ushered (Y/N) to grab the gifts beside the crypt as she nodded, Enid grabbing onto the cake as she unboxed it, (Y/N) by her side.

Enid flicked flames onto the candles lighting them up as (Y/N) managed to grab ahold of the gifts, the two then eventually walked through the door and saw the people singing happy birthday to Wednesday as (Y/N) and Enid came along, Enid smiled happily as they all came together and sang happy birthday to the black-haired girl who stood there in shock.

Wednesday immediately looked down at Thing who wore a small black party hat, a look of embarrassment and anger radiating through her. "I should have known you were behind this." Wednesday growled, her light flashed towards Thing, "What part of 'no party under the penalty of death' do you not understand?" The girl scoffed in disbelief, making everyone look at Wednesday.

"I thought my cake design was pretty inspired." (Y/N) laughed heartedly, as the cake had three layers, covered with black fondant having white fondant beautifully detailed along the cake making it look like a spider's web, along with the widow itself at the top in a threatening pose. The words 'Happy 16th Birthday Wednesday' was in a dark yet noticeable red which Pluto admired, making Wednesday's eyes widen slightly at the design, but postured herself.

"(Y/N) wouldn't let me have a pink balloon on it," Enid sighed sadly, "She said that it'd ruin it." The girl fake-pouted making (Y/N) shake her head with a small smirk as she jokingly nudged her shoulder, as (Y/N) placed the gifts down to the side, "Why don't you make a wish?" Enid suggested as the room quietened down for a moment awkwardly until the candles went out. "Ah-- shoot--" Enid whispered as (Y/N) pulled out the lighter from earlier and lit up the candles once more as the students watched Wednesday walk to a wall of which its stones walls were engraved.

"Wait, it's Latin." Wednesday began as (Y/N)'s eyes flickered between Enid and the others, and then at Wednesday as (Y/N) hesitantly walked up to Wednesday.

(Y/N) translated using her mind, mummbling aloud for everyone to hear, in sync with Wednesday, "Fire will rain... when I rise." Wednesday's eyes widened looking at (Y/N) who had a dumfounded expression, but widened at the sudden memory from days ago remembering the burnt out field that still stood there. "Okay-- that's not really a wish--" Enid studdered lightly.

"The first part of that was burnt on Nevermore's lawn." Wednesday uttered, "It can't be a coincidence." Wednesday determined, "Wait, we're never eating that cake, are we?" Ajax questioned behind Enid, as she looked at him as he had sad eyes as the two stood there, looking at the wall.

(Y/N) placed her arm on her shoulder with a look of concern as Wednesday would then hesitantly touch the wall, her black-coloured fingernails gently brushing the words until she eventually stopped making (Y/N) concerned for a moment until (Y/N)'s eyes widened along with Wednesday's as the two were hollered in an unknown area.

Whispering could be heard around the two as Wednesday laid in (Y/N)'s arm, as Wednesday woke up to her relative whispering to her, "Crackstone is coming." The girl warned as Wednesday immediately woke up to the unfamiliar area, (Y/N)'s eyes still closed, probably from the impact from teleporting there.

Wednesday raised her head, seeing her relation, Goody Addams stood behind large black gates, along with Astoria as it towered over the two, making Wednesday curious, as she immediately shook (Y/N) who was in a chaotic state next to her.

"(Y/N)-- (Y/N)--" She shook her awake making her jolt up at the sudden touch, "Come--" Wednesday pulled her up, as Pluto's mind started pondering from standing up quickly, "Wha--" (Y/N) was cut off from seeing her's and Wednesday's relative who stood there at the gate.

"Astoria." Wednesday muttered, (Y/N) whispered, "Goody."

"You're the raven in our bloodline." The two muttered at once making (Y/N)'s and Wednesday's eyes flicker to one another.

"Wednesday." A voice called out to her side as Goody Addams and Astoria (L/N) were next to them making (Y/N) flinch slightly at the sudden teleportation.

"I was told you could teach me how to control my ability." Wednesday again as (Y/N) and Astoria stared at each other, making (Y/N) shuffle around uncomfortably behnind Wednesday, as Goody and Wednesday talked to each other.

Pluto couldn't help but feel this bone-chilling emotion that pulsed throughout her body as Astoria's blood red eyes bore into her with her predatory eyes.

(Y/N) looked to where Goody and Wednesday looked, "To stop Crackstone, this place you must seek." Goody began, as Wednesday stood next to (Y/N), Astoria's eyes never taking off (Y/N) which made (Y/N) byfar uncomfortable.

"Do you always speak in riddles?" Wednesday asked, "Do you always seek simple answers?" Goody gritted her teeth, facing her descendant as Astoria's eyes were finally off (Y/N) as she eyed the girl that stood next to her, keeping quiet.

"The path of a raven is a solitary one," Goody began, her eyes flickering to (Y/N) for a moment, "But a raven is nothing without it's unkindness." She began, as (Y/N)'s eyes flickered to Goody for a moment, "Sorry?" The girl asked, "Sorry-- It's just that this place seems oddly familiar." (Y/N) acknowledged, examining every detail of it.

"Is that suppose to scare me?" Wednesday raised an eyebrow at (Y/N) for a moment, "It should." Goody replied to the dark haired girl's comment before the two girl's disappeared by the soft chuckle of Astoria, ending up in the dark crypt oncemore.

(Y/N) and Wednesday were eventually taken to Wednesday's shared dormitory, her eyes forever closed as she was thankfully carried there by the help of her friend, Ajax.

(Y/N) was taken to Enid's and Wednesday's dormitory since her one was quite far, Wednesday was up all night sketching the unfamiliar gates of the large house as Thing crawled upon her shoulder, "Careful, that's my cold shoulder." The girl spat bitterly at Thing as he crawled down to her desk as (Y/N) slept on Enid's bed.

"Don't be mad at Thing, the whole thing was my idea." Enid smiled, "I believe everyone deserves to be celebrated on their birthday." Enid smiled once more, "I prefer to be vilified." The girl determined, continuing to sketch.

"What happened? It looked like the two of you had a seizure." Enid questioned sadly, looking at (Y/N) who slept in her clothes from the night before. "I wasn't that lucky." Wednesday muttered, her eyes still fixated on the paper, "Can I at least get some kudos before pulling one over you?" Enid rolled her eyes playfully at her roommate which made Wednesday stop shading in, and scoffed in disbelief, "The subterfuge was impressive." Wednesday paused, never daring to make eye contact with Enid.

Wednesday looked over to see Thing pull out a large and heavy box from under the bed, making her drop her stuff and walk over to him, "May your 16th Birthday be as sour and misery-filled as your desire." Wednesday read the letter out loud, making Enid smile widely.

"Your ever-doting, Mother and Father." Wednesday finished, opening up the bag which revealed various things, as well as roadkill pests, which immediately made Enid grossed out and whine out loud making (Y/N) wake up, startled.

"Ack-- What'd I miss?--" (Y/N) groaned, using her mechanical arm to push her up, rubbing her eyes with her left hand in the meantime, as she looked at Enid who came over to (Y/N), "Oh-- You're awake--" Enid blinked, noticing the (H/C) haired girl as she went to grab the ack-wrapped up gift that sat on the nightstand next to (Y/N).

"Uh-huh..." (Y/N) hummed, adverting her gaze at the blonde-haired girl, "Well, come on-- We need to give Wednesday our presents." Enid whispered to (Y/N) which made her smile slightly with a nod. Enid giggled slightly, grabbing a hold of the present with a crunch, as she made her way toward Wednesday as the two talked to each other, as Wednesday hesitantly opened the gift, making eye contact with (Y/N) for a moment as she came over, her hand in her pocket.

"I made one for (Y/N) not too long ago," She continued, "She has a white one since I'm not too sure what her color pattern is." Enid shrugged as she put her snood on, her blonde locks bouncy around as (Y/N) shrugged sheepishly. "And uh-- Here's my gift--" (Y/N) began, handing her a red box, covered with a dark-red color, making Wednesday look at (Y/N) with a skeptical look.

"Well, go on." (Y/N) smiled reassuringly as Wednesday placed down her snood, and slowly opened up the small box, and to her complete surprise, it showed a beautiful ring, which made her eyes widen, and her mouth open slightly.

She blinked twice, looking up at (Y/N) who had a small smile, "Do you like it?" (Y/N) asked as Wednesday gently grabbed ahold of it and slipped it on her ring finger, admiring the small rubies that looked like they glared throughout her soul which made her smile lightly, making Enid notice.

Wednesday fidgeted with the head of the skull on the ring and looked up at (Y/N). "I really do like it, thank you." Wednesday looked up at (Y/N) with a smile as she put the box in her pocket, "The pleasure is all mine." (Y/N) smiled at the girl who had a small smile of her own.

The dark-haired girl quickly realized her actions and immediately stopped smiling, stiffening at the sudden action she did, making (Y/N) chuckle lightly at her actions. Enid watched between the two smugly snapping photos of the two.

Wednesday stood in front of the burnt out field, examining the words as (Y/N) came up beside her in a suitable home-like attire. "You saw that vision, didn't you, Wednesday?" (Y/N) asked, her hands in her pocket while doing so as Wednesday's eyes never darted to (Y/N) in the meantime.

Wednesday would still look as she nodded with a small hum, her hands shuffling around in her pocket uncomfortably unsure of what to say next. "Do you still think I'm the monster?" (Y/N) asked with a sad look plastering on her face as Wednesday would stiffen slightly, making (Y/N) notice. "I haven't ruled it out." Wednesday admitted, looking at her ring finger for a moment, then side glanced toward (Y/N) for a slight second.

(Y/N) was taken aback from Wednesday's statement as she fiddled around with her fingers, as she shakily managed to utter out, "When you change your mind, and you want my help, you know where to find me." (Y/N) uttered with a toothy grin as she left, leaving Wednesday there with a saddened look, (Y/N) never looking back in the meantime.

(Y/N) clutched on her bag as she walked to the carpark after her encounter with Wednesday. She looked up to see Larissa Weems glare down at her making her slightly uncomfortable as she just shrugged it aside. (Y/N) immediately used her keys to open her car as she threw her bag at he back and drove her way to work.

(Y/N) pulled up, grabbed her stuff, and locked her way entering the coffee shop getting hit by the familiar coffee smell as lingered through the Weathervane. (Y/N) was in the back preparing to come on shift as Tyler and her would switch every 1 hour, and have a 20 minute break in the process.

(Y/N) was brewing some coffee for customers, her back turned towards the counter until the bell rang, causing her attention. The girl was working from the back, she turned on her heel holding two cups of black coffee which was strong under her nose. "Hello, Welcome to Weathervane, Can I get your or--" Pluto was cut off, seeing Wednesday there as she placed down the cups to the side of her, "A quad over ice, I presume?" (Y/N)'d attitude changed into a more relaxed one as she grabbed her notebook and wrote it down as Wednesday nodded.

The two didn't speak to each other as (Y/N) placed their cups on a silver plate and walked over to them, handing their coffee to them with a small, but pleasant smile. Wednesday examined her every move in the distance, to the point she didn't notice that her book was upside down. (Y/N) walked back to the counter, beginning to brew Wednesday coffee as Tyler came out of the backroom. "Hey, (Y/N)." He began, gaining the girl's attention, "You can go to Nevermore now if you want, we're open for a short time today." He finished making (Y/N) nod, as Tyler finished the coffee then walked to Wednesday and slipped her, her coffee which had 'Happy Birthday' on it.

(Y/N) was cleaning up the area before she went into the back for her break, but couldn't help but stare at the two in the distance, which indeed made her quite envious at the brown-haired male as (Y/N) didn't notice that a glass cup she smashed the cup with her mechanical hand, gaining everyone's attention.

"Sorry-- Sorry--" (Y/N) mumbled an apology several times embarrassed by the mess she caused as she quickly went to find a dust and pan and quickly swept up the mess, putting them in the rubbish, and fleeting to the backrooms with a heavy sigh of frustration, taking off her apron, throwing it on the rack next to her.

"Finally." (Y/N) grunted tiredly, grabbing her bag and keys, walking out of there never wanting to look back as she drove back to the heavily crowded school.

(Y/N) wanted to get things off her mind and intended on going to her art studio.

(Y/N) wore a plain (F/C) jersey that was stained by oil paints, and more as loud music blasted throughout her headphones humming along to the tune as she flicked paint onto the canvas with her robotic hand, as the door would slightly creak open to reveal Wednesday, alarming (Y/N) as she stood there puzzled.

(Y/N) took off her headphones, her music playing distinctively as Wednesday didn't make eye contact with her as she muttered, "I need your help." she began, as (Y/N) raised an eyebrow, "With what?" (Y/N) asked, as Wednesday handed (Y/N) a poorly sketched out gate making (Y/N) look at her with realization. "Oh." (Y/N) muttered, examining the paper in front of her as she turned off the music. "We saw that in the vision, remember? Do you recognize it?" Wednesday tried to spike a conversation at the gnawing silence.

"Mhm." (Y/N) hummed, "I *have* seen it before-- like a photo or something." (Y/N) shrugged, "It looked something like that." (Y/N) pointed at a drawing she drew. "I tried drawing Astoria and Goody, but I suck." The girl muttered, as Wednesday's eyes widened, having a close look at it.

"OH--" (Y/N) eyes widened, "Now I remember," (Y/N) placed her balled-up fist on her palm in thought, "It's the old Gates' mansion" (Y/N) remembered, "I remember doing a project about them-- That's why I couldn't remember." (Y/N) chuckled proudly, suddenly remembering the slight memory as she leaned against the table as Wednesday ran her fingers along the lines, and the exquisite details that (Y/N) added in.

(Y/N) couldn't help but looked around the room in a panic, noticing that Thing had disappeared, of which she suspected that he wandered around. (Y/N) noticed Thing stand near the oddly tall canvas which made (Y/N)'s eyes widen, "Hey-- Don't touch th--" (Y/N) was cut off as Thing tapped, gaining Wednesday's attention as he ripped the sheet off the painting.

(Y/N) looked down in embarrassment as Wednesday looked over at the canvas with a startled expression, as it showed a beautifully detailed portrait of Wednesday

Addams herself, her cello delicately in her cold hands, eyes full of concentration. Wednesday would walk up to the canvas, her eyes still wide at the canvas in font of her as she stopped.

(Y/N) cleared her throat as she walked behind Wednesday, "It was supposed to be your birthday present--" (Y/N) stuffed her hands in her pocket, with a tired chuckle. "But I was a few days late-- and I still waned to give you a present so--" (Y/N) tried to fumble out words but looked down with a tired look.

"I could hear you up there playing, and ever since outreach day..." (Y/N) hummed lightly, as she reached out her hand, as the canvas soon began to play a soft melody, Wednesday still in shock. "Sorry--" (Y/N) muttered, looking down at the ground as Wednesday glanced at (Y/N) for one last time as she immediately walked out of there, along with Thing, leaving (Y/N) all alone to herself.

The night after (Y/N)'s and Wednesday's encounter, the two barely talked as (Y/N) was at the same old job she worked at, gaining money just to save up, despite having a massive fortune.

(Y/N) walked over with Sheriff Galpin's black coffee placing it in front of him, "Here you go." (Y/N) looked with a pleasant smile, looking through the glass she saw the Mayor walk toward the shop making her send him a small wave.

Her smile soon faded when she saw a car at full speed crashing into him as he flew across the car, making her drop the silver plate she held in her hand, her eyes widening. The Sheriff's eyes also did, as he yelled, "NO!" The man immediately ran outside to where the man's body was, (Y/N) still in great shock and disbelief.

The man then looked at the girl who came out of the Sheriff's boot as she looked down at the ground, as (Y/N) looked between the two before turning on her heel, running to the backroom to try and calm herself down, which eventually worked, as she just wanted to go back to her dormitory.

"This can't be happening." (Y/N) muttered to herself, slamming her car door shut, since she spent another hour working at the Weathervane, as she heard the news that the school was on lockdown, so she made the most of it, before being locked away. She walked along the gravel footpath, muttering to herself as she had witnessed another one's death.

(Y/N)'s mind was clouded with dreadful thoughts that she didn't see Wednesday coming as she accidentally bumped into her, alarming the girl. "Sorry." (Y/N) apologized hesitantly, gaining her posture as she still had her eyes fixated on the ground, brushing past Wednesday, never making eye contact with Wednesday, which seemingly made her sad.

(Y/N) eventually walked back to her dorm as she noticed that her roommate wasn't there although with a dejected sigh she kicked her shoes off her feet, throwing her bag on her chair as she tiredly slumped down on her bed, hugging her pillow tightly.

(Y/N) bit onto her lips, trying to forget about both Rowan's and Mayor Walker's death, but couldn't get over it. It felt like a tough current pulling her out to the sea, small tears threatening to fall out of her eyes until she heard a small but faint knock ruined her intrusive mind.

With a small sniffle, she wiped her tears away, digging her hand in her pockets, until she eventually opened up the door. "Mother?" (Y/N) looked up at the familiar red head woman, her eyes still full of tears, she honestly felt like she could drop on the ground.

The woman's soft and charismatic smile fell seeing the state of her step daughter disheartening state, "(Y/N)? Are you okay?" The woman began, her eyes widening as her voice laced in panic and sadness she felt for her daughter. The woman immediately pulled in (Y/N) for a hug, making (Y/N) shudder in sadness, breaking down.

"I witnessed another one." (Y/N) voice cracked, "I'm not ready for this." The girl cried, hugging onto her mother as her eye's widened, fearful for her. "Honey-- it's alright." The woman reassured, her eyebrows creasing in sadness for her step-daughter's current state, (Y/N) held to her tightly until the two broke apart.

"I'm sorry, I really am." (Y/N) apologized, looking at the ground, tears eventually stopped, her eyes forever red making the woman concerned, "(Y/N), why are you crying?" The woman's sweet voice began as (Y/N) flinched slightly at the question, "I told you, did I?" (Y/N) sighed lightly, beginning to raise her head up at her step mother who had a twisted look of guilt and sadness.

"I came here to tell you if you could go to the shop for some stuff for the cafeteria-- But that can wait until tomorrow night." The woman began, patting her step-daughter's shoulder. "Okay then-- is that what you were in here for?" (Y/N) questioned making the woman nod with a small-sad smile. "Okay then... I'll get them tomorrow night." (Y/N) gave the woman a bittersweet smile before closing the door, the woman placed her hand on it before the door closed.

"Goodnight, (Y/N)." The woman finished as (Y/N) nodded, "You too." (Y/N) smiled softly before closing the door with a soft clank, and was once again met with the long gnawing silence.

It was eventually the night after the previous one, as (Y/N) was on her way to the local Jericho supermarket with the permission of Larissa Weems herself.

The cold air bit onto her although she wore a long (F/C) trench coat, a (F/C) tank top, a pair of (F/C) jeans, and to top it all off she wore her soft white everlasting snood to go with it. (Y/N) gathered her keys and whistled a small song that came to her mind as she jumped out her dormitory window, floating down to her car.

(Y/N) pulled out the long list that her step-mother had given to her, "Dayum." She muttered to herself before she shrugged before opening up the car door, closing it with a soft but loud thud. (Y/N) then started up her car before pulling out of the school.

Her music was boosted out loud as she drove as a smooth pace, not fast like she'd usually comprehend. Dusk painted the lovely sky, a full moon to go with it, leaving a sickening hue of all sorts of colors. (Y/N) eventually ended up at the shop, as there waited a man who was slightly plumped, who wore a charismatic smile.

"Hello there young lady." The man smiled, "Are you the one named (Y/N), perhaps?" The man questioned, (Y/N) nodded. "Yes, I am." (Y/N) nodded with a small but hesitant smile. "Ah-- Okay then. It's just a young lady named Marilyn ought to call me." He beckoned, "She ordered a ton of crates. Aha." The man stifled a gruff laugh.

"Anyways, come with me, kiddo." He ushered making (Y/N) follow the man who seemed like an employee.

The man led (Y/N) to a room filled with a few large crates of food, the familiar scent of salary hitting her nose. "Here ya go young lady." The man shrugged, "Do you need help with carrying them?" The man questioned looking at (Y/N) who held her arms up, "Ah-- No-- no thank you, Sir. I'm sure that I'll be able to handle this." Pluto smiled at the man as he nodded at her.

"Alright then, Good luck with that!" The man bid her a small goodbye before leaving the multicolored eyed girl there to deal with it.

What seemed like hours, although a few minutes, (Y/N) eventually stacked the heavy boxes of food at the back of her car.

"Here ya go, Miss." The man came back with a card register, once (Y/N) had finished stacking the boxes in her car. The girl grasped onto her wallet in her pocket, as flicked out her credit card as the man tapped a few numbers on there as it showed with the price, *'2550$'*

(Y/N) looked at her card and then at the man, as she used her pay wave on it, getting accepted. "Thank you kind lady." The man smiled, "Have a safe trip back home!" The man waved off, making (Y/N) smile. "Thank you, and you too!" (Y/N) smiled widely before hopping back in her car as the two had parted ways, starting her engine she drove back to the academy.

(Y/N) decided to take a much longer and different route back to the academy, just to get a little breath of fresh air, before being tormented and enclosed back at the school.

(Y/N) was driving in her car, her fingers tapped rhythmically along the beat, her hands on the steering wheel until she eventually saw the familiar sight of the Gates mansion. (Y/N) then head a few screams and a loud creature snarl, which mildly made her concerned. "What the f--" She was cut off by the loud roar that belonged to the monster itself, as it came from that direction, the abandoned mansion that stood there.

(Y/N)'s eyes widened in realization that from Wednesday's and (Y/N)'s conversation earlier, she realized that it could've been here conflicted in this, and quickly speed up, until skidding to a stop, immediately running into the gates, forcing them open as she immediately ran around the place, seeing a few flashlights in the distance.

(Y/N)'s eyes widened when she saw Tyler's state, looking between Enid, Wednesday, and the boy himself. "Where'd you come from?" Wednesday stared with wide eyes at (Y/N) who panted tiredly, (Y/N)'s eyes widened as she quickly tore off her snood giving it to Tyler as blood gushed out of him. "Here, give him this--" (Y/N) muttered.

"What happened to him?" (Y/N) questioned, as everyone just stared at (Y/N) with wide eyes, making (Y/N) look at them in a confused and concerned manner.

They all decided to go to Tyler's house as Wednesday was bandaging up Tyler's clawed chest as Enid sat close next to (Y/N). Tyler winced at the slightest touch, making (Y/N) wince also. "Thanks, Doc." Tyler gazed down at Wednesday, making (Y/N)'s eyes flinch slightly, looking elsewhere, her lips pressing into a thin line.

"Not to make this about me, but I am having a full-blown panic attack now." Enid's eyes full of horror making (Y/N) look down at her with a saddened look, rubbing her back in circles comfortingly. "We need to get back before Weems realizes we're gone--" Enid began until she was cut off by the head sheriff opening the door. "I should've just went back--" (Y/N) mumbled to herself, as the man just stood there, this eyes looking at everyone in disbelief, but mostly terror for his son.

"What the hell happened?" The man began, as Wednesday stood up alarmed. "This was you, wasn't it?" The man began as he charged toward Wednesday as (Y/N) stood up quickly, knocking her chair over. Tyler then stood in front of Wednesday before anything nasty could happen, "Wait-- Dad-- Please. I'm okay." Tyler began.

(Y/N) hesitantly sat back down, looking between the three people as Enid looked at her, her eyebrows creasing. "Sheriff. I understand that you're upset, but I think there's something you need to see." Wednesday began with a stern and proper manner.

(Y/N) drove back to the school, notifying the Sheriff that she was aloud to grab a box of heavy crates for the local cafeteria.

(Y/N) eventually drove back to the school, Enid by her side on the passenger seat. "(Y/N)? Was it you?" Enid shuddered at the thought as (Y/N) raised an eyebrow, "What do you mean?" The girl began, side glancing at her with her (E/C) colored iris at the girl as the ride back was slow, and steady.

No music played, the only thing audible was the tires hitting the concrete floor. "Nevermind," The girl began as (Y/N) hummed to herself, "Who am I kidding. Of course the monster isn't you." (Y/N) flinched slightly, her eyes never leaving the road. "Are you calling me a monster?"

(Y/N) joked slightly, looking down as a small smirk formed on her face.

"No! No-- Of course not." Enid waved her hands in front of her face, "You're my friend-- More than anything!" Enid fumbled over her words, "You honestly don't look-- or act like a monster." Enid fidgeted with her fingers, (Y/N) let out a warm sigh with a chuckle.

"It's fine, honestly. I've been called worse, I guess." (Y/N) hummed with a small soft smile, Enid's eyes widened. "Tell me more." Enid began, slowly relaxing in the seat as (Y/N) smiled down at the ground with a small smile. "If you insist." (Y/N) shrugged.

"I've been called a tiger." (Y/N) let out a small disbelief laugh that was more like a scoff. "I guess they meant it in a cold-disheartening way. I'm not too sure." (Y/N) began, her long and slender fingers gently held onto the steering wheel. "Honestly (Y/N), I don't think of you as a raging tiger or something like that." Enid shrugged with a small smile.

"You're a friend, more than a tiger." She continued, "Although, you symbolize as one. Tiger's represents wisdom and prosperity, you're all that." Enid finished with a wide smile, making (Y/N) look down at her with a small but soft smile, "Thanks, Enid. I really needed that." (Y/N) thanked, her smile never fading as she pulled up to the old-fashioned school.

(Y/N) eventually pulled up to the car park, as heavy rain poured, but she was thankfully helped by a few staff members who took inside some of the crates that held vegetables, fruit, and more.

"(Y/N), are you alright?" Enid asked, snapping Pluto out of her day-dream like state. "Yeah-- Yeah. I'm fine." (Y/N) muttered as she noticed that there were no more crates in her boot, as she closed it with a heavy thud, locking her car in the process.

"Thanks for letting me come with you too, (Y/N). You're a real life-saver." Enid smiled at the taller girl as she looked down at her with a closed-eye smile "Ah-- It's no problem. Thanks for keeping accompanying me." (Y/N) thanked as the two walked near the quad, "Also (Y/N)-- I hope it's not an issue for you... But I was wondering if we could swap dormitories-- for now at least." Enid began, looking at the ground with a saddened expression knowing that she'd get rejected.

"Oh, If it doesn't bother you than sure--" (Y/N) was cut off by Enid's short arms wrap around her waist, alarming (Y/N) halting her to a stop. "Thank you, thank you, thank you!" Enid cried aloud, as (Y/N) hesitantly wrapped her arms around her comfortingly, "You're such a good friend, (Y/N). I swear it!" Enid swore as (Y/N) smiled down at her as the two tore apart, "I'll go pack my things." Enid smiled,

"Is it okay if you talk to your mother about it?" Enid asked, as (Y/N) nodded.

"Of course, I'll inform her immediately." (Y/N) acknowledged as Enid smiled widely, "Go pack yours in the meantime, (Y/N)." The girl began, nudging (Y/N)'s shoulder as (Y/N) nodded with a small smile. "Sure." (Y/N) began as the two parted ways.

(Y/N) flew back to her dormitory and stood at the large door frame, "Hey, Yoko. I'm switching dorms with Enid, for now at least." (Y/N) shrugged walking over to her bed where her suitcase was, as she grabbed a few clothes and other stuff that meant well to her as she gently placed them in her bag. "When will you come back?" Enid questioned making (Y/N) look behind her slightly.

"I'll come back in a few nights." (Y/N) smiled, finally finished packing her stuff, as she messaged Enid throughout her mind telling her that her mother accepted the two girl's request, as she was only aloud to stay there for a few nights.

(Y/N) took awhile to get her things all ready and packed, until she saw Enid come into the room. "Oh, that was quick." (Y/N) began, her eyes widening as she grabbed onto her (F/C) suitcase all ready to go. "You alright, Enid?" (Y/N) questioned, concerned as she let out a small huff. "Yeah, I am. I just got into an argument with Wednesday." Enid began as she slumped down on the comfortable bed with a sigh of frustration.

(Y/N) let out a hearty chuckle before walking to the door, "I guess I'll see you guys later." (Y/N) smiled, exchanging dorm keys with Enid and herself, before closing the door behind her with a loud thud, beginning to walk to Ophelia Hall.

The walk was quiet and deafening, the only thing that could be heard was the heavy rain pour, along with the thunder roar within its clouds. (Y/N) eventually stood in front of Enid's and Wednesday's dormitory, until getting the courage to open it with a small clack, and in the distance she saw Wednesday bundled up in a ball, sitting in front of the spider web window with a sad look on her face.

"Wednesday?" (Y/N)'s voice echoed, as lightning would strike within the distance, alarming Wednesday as she flinched slightly at the familiar voice. A small brown-colored jewelry box fell out of her bag, a soft musical box playing in the meantime, as a few pictures fell out, which made Wednesday look down slightly curious at the pictures.

"Nice to see you too." (Y/N) muttered to Wednesday, walking over to Enid's side of the room, placing her suitcase on the side on the bed, beginning to unpack her stuff, as Wednesday's eyes would widen at the photos, which made (Y/N) slightly skeptical.

Wednesday kept silent as she gathered the small jewelry box, along with the photos and walked to her desk, placing them aside, as she typed on her type writer.

Once (Y/N) was finished unpacking, she decided to walk over to Wednesday as she was busy typing her book. "Hey-- Wednesday..." (Y/N) began, shuffling uncomfortably, gaining the black-haired girl's attention. "I just wanted to apologize for the painting I did of you-- It really was a late birthday gift--" (Y/N) fumbled over her words, continuing. "If it makes you comfortable-- I just wanted to let you know that I threw it away--" (Y/N) finished, looking down at Wednesday.

Wednesday's facial features relaxed once she heard those words from (Y/N), her eyes meeting (Y/N)'s (E/C) and (F/C) ones. "It's fine." Wednesday began, returning her attention to her type writer, her slender fingers typing along it. "Ah-- Okay then." (Y/N) bowed down in respect, as she walked to Enid's side of the room, and slipped underneath the sheets, closing her eyes in the process.

Chapter Seven, If You Don't Woe Me by Now.

3RD PERSON'S POINT OF VIEW.

A funeral was held for the Mayor himself, as he had tragically passed on.

Many people wore black as Wednesday and (Y/N) stood close to each other, (Y/N) having a look of dread and sadness. "How tragic." (Y/N) muttered to Wednesday as she held onto a black umbrella between the two, as Wednesday couldn't help but keep quiet to herself.

A moment of silence was held upon the large amount of people there, as Wednesday side glanced at a covered up figure, making (Y/N) notice as the odd figure dashed away within the woods making Wednesday chase after it. "Wait Wednesday-- Your umbr--" (Y/N) tried to make out words, but fumbled slight, "ella..." (Y/N) finished, looking at the girl who disappeared off into the distance, as the hollow rain disappeared making (Y/N) flicker her eyes off into the distance until turning off on her heel, walking back to her car, flicking water on her palms before leaving the cemetery to drive back to the school.

(Y/N) was laying in Enid's bed with her classic Twilight book, as she saw Wednesday enter the room with a puzzled expression.

"There you are," (Y/N) closed her book, looking at Wednesday who glanced at (Y/N) for a moment with a short nod, before walking to her desk, flicking on her old-fashioned record player, as classical guitar would play elegantly, as Wednesday typed on her type-writer, as it would clack then and there, with a small ding. (Y/N) in the meantime would shrug, continuing to read her book.

Wednesday would open up her drawer, grabbing out the beautiful small jewelry box, examining every detail of it, as she looked behind her, seeing the (H/C) haired girl, posing quite elegantly in a nice posture, her eyes fixated on her book her held with her soft slender fingers, as she looked up, with a small '*Hm?*'.

"Can I help you?" (Y/N) asked, raising an eyebrow, which immediately made Wednesday shook her head in the process, eventually closing the brown jewelry box, and put it back in the drawer that was opened, closing it with a small thud.

(Y/N) would look down with a small frown of confusion, continuing to read as Enid came to the door, opening it as Wednesday stood up to go near Enid who looked at (Y/N) reading her book, her knuckled gently pushed against her cheek.

"Hi." Enid began, a small but hesitant smile coming over her face. "Sorry, I figured you were at Mayor Walker's wake." Enid began, walking toward Wednesday, (Y/N) glancing up at the two for a second. "As soon as the dirt hits the coffin, I'm out." Wednesday began, glaring at her old roommate.

"I can't seem to find my bottle of silver moon nail polish," Enid began, hesitantly walking forward, "Do you mind if I look around?" Enid asked Wednesday as (Y/N) eventually closed her book, and sat up on the bed, looking at Enid with a small smile, as the music would stop, allowing Wednesday to turn to face Enid.

"Yoko's hosting a mani-pedi party for her crew." Enid tried to acknowledge, having a look on her night stand, Wednesday and Enid walking at the same pace, the opposite side of the room. "This is the third time in 24 hours you've forgotten something." Wednesday began, crossing her arms, facing the two girls.

"So, how's everything going?" Enid fumbled, opening up the nightstand, trying to look for her silver nail polish. "Solitude suits me." Wednesday began, glaring down at (Y/N) for a moment as she had a dumbfounded look. "Although (Y/N) is here, she doesn't cause any annoying distractions, to the point I'm almost finished with my novel." Wednesday glared back at Enid.

"Was I an annoying distraction?" Enid asked with a tiresome look, closing the small drawer that was in front of her, making (Y/N) pressed her lips into a thin line. What a wave of nostalgia.

"You definitely had some annoying habits." Wednesday glared, "Such as?" Enid asked, "You giggle when you text, which is a 24/7 addiction." Wednesday glared continuously, her blank look still the same, like any other time. "Well, At least it's not a migraine-inducing typewriter hammering into my head." Enid began, taunting Wednesday as she did to her not too long ago.

"When not grinding your canines, you growl in your sleep." Wednesday began, "As supposed to late night cello solos?" Enid began, "You over-commit to activities, then complain about them." Wednesday bit back, "I'd take that over your obsession with all things creepy." Enid began, stepping forward with her hands behind her back.

Wednesday stepped forward as well, "You could gas an entire village with the amount of perfume you spritz." Wednesday glared, "That's just off the top of my head." Enid's mouth quivered in anger and sadness, "Guess I'm lucky with the new bestie that doesn't try find ways to endanger literally everybody she comes into contact with." Enid finished, her eyes painted with sadness as fury.

"In fact, Yoko and I are so in sync, that she's begging me to be her new roomie." Enid began making (Y/N) look at Enid with a dreaded look, as Wednesday's eyebrows raised at the sudden request. "Permanently." Enid finished, as the two glared at each other as Enid looked at (Y/N) for a moment, then at Wednesday who turned on her heel, her back toward Enid.

"Don't let me hold you back." Wednesday promoted angrily, "Enjoy your solitude, Wednesday!" Enid stormed out, "It's not solitude if (Y/N)'s here." Enid closed the door roughly, making it slam shut, making (Y/N) flinch.

"Well that was calming." (Y/N) muttered to herself, shaking her head as she began to read her book.

(Y/N) eventually fell asleep while reading her, which made Wednesday notice as she hesitantly walked to (Y/N), grabbing ahold of her book in her hands making her gasp lightly, waking up as their faces were inches apart.

"What are you doing--" (Y/N)'s eyes widened as Wednesday sighed grabbing her book, "I was planning on placing your book aside, yet you woke up." Wednesday acknowledged in a proper manner, "But why were you so close to my--" (Y/N) was cut off by Wednesday.

"I told you, (Y/N). Don't be stubborn." Wednesday glared down at (Y/N) as she walked away from (Y/N). "What I don't get is why are you so mean to me--" (Y/N) scoffed slightly, then looked down with sadness, rubbing the corner of her lips with the back of her hand as Wednesday turned on her heel to face (Y/N).

"Are you that desperate to know?" Wednesday with a hint of anger, glaring at (Y/N).

(Y/N) eventually sat up on Enid's bed, a hint of irritation lacing though her voice although she spoke in a calm manner.

"I've been on your side since day one," Pluto mumbled, "I literally saved life..." (Y/N) began, her voice laced in sadness more than irritation. "I felt like walking on a tight rope telling Larissa that some monster killed Rowan." (Y/N) began, crossing her arms.

"And what did I get in return-- Nothing!" (Y/N) raised her voice, tiresomely at Wednesday who flinched in the meantime, "And with *our* ancestors knowing each other... even *our* parents! Does that not mean anything to you?" (Y/N) questioned, her eye's widening with disbelief, anger, self-pity.

"I feel like I'm being lied to, Wednesday." (Y/N) huffed is sadness, gnawing the inside of her cheek slightly, putting her hands on her face tiredly as Wednesday stood there with wide eyes, before it eventually turned into a stone-cold glare.

"Fine. You want honesty? Here it is." Wednesday began, making (Y/N) raise her head, her hands still resting on her jaw. "Every time the monster's attacked, you've been right there." Wednesday motioned making (Y/N)'s eyes widen, "Starting with Rowan at the Harvest Festival." She began, "Then on out reach day, you arrived just minutes after the monster disappeared, yet you say you didn't see it." She listed.

"I didn't realize proximity was a crime." (Y/N) replied back, baffled. "Then there's your drawing obsession." She continued, "You have drawn the monster dozens of times, yet you've never seen it, or so you claim." She finished, making (Y/N) look at Wednesday with a look of sadness wash over her.

"You even drew where it lived. Then when Eugene went to go investigate, you tried to kill him so he wouldn't spill your secret." The girl continued, as (Y/N) stood up and scoffed in disbelief, "You even had the audacity to sit next to him in that hospital room." Wednesday began, raising her voice louder, as (Y/N) walked up to Wednesday with a saddened look on her face. "You think I would hurt Eugene?" (Y/N) scoffed with mixed emotions.

"Let's not forget your oh-so-convenient appearance after Tyler had been attacked at the Gates mansion." Wednesday began, as (Y/N) would hung her head low. "If I am the monster," (Y/N) muttered, "Why haven't I killed you?" (Y/N) looked at Wednesday as glossed in her multi-colored eyes, making Wednesday down slightly.

"Because for some reason I cannot fathom or indulge, you seem to like me." Wednesday continued to look down whilst saying that as (Y/N)'s expression seemed to get much more sadder, which soon was replaced by a look of fury and anger.

"And I can't believe I *did*." (Y/N) snapped back bitterly as she looked down at Wednesday with hatred, making Wednesday's eyes widen as (Y/N) shook her head in disbelief, walking out of the room back to her art studio.

Wednesday stood on the spot, her hands shaking. Wednesday repeated to herself, to not cry internally. Wednesday stood in the same spot for what seemed like a few minutes as she looked down at the ground, feeling useless as a few specs of salt-water came running down her cheeks, hitting the wood that stood beneath her, realizing what she did. Her soft purple pigmented lips trembled in the meantime.

A thump noise occurred behind her, making her jolt slightly as she quickly wiped her tears, turning behind her to face her Uncle Fester. "How long have you been lurking?" Wednesday asked, her dark and mesmerizing expression coming back on her face. "Not long enough," Her uncle chortled a laugh.

"Yowza!" He exclaimed, his smile faded seeing the state of his niece, "Are you alright, Wednesday?" He asked, concerned for his niece, as she looked at him with a slight hesitant look. "Yes. Of course." She stiffened slightly in a proper manner, as the curiosity fell off the man quick.

"Now must we get going?" Wednesday began, roughly changing the subject, negotiating him to the door, "Likewise." The man smile heartedly as the two left to go to the secret-hidden library that belonged to the Nightshades.

Once they retrieved the run-down journal, they quickly made it back to their dormitory, (Y/N) nowhere in sight which made Wednesday slightly disappointed.

Wednesday did some research reading the novel of the monster, of which is described as a Hyde. Wednesday found out that that she wasn't dealing with one monster, but two.

Wednesday stopped reading as she heard a knock at the door, which she immediately thought was (Y/N) as she quickly closed the book, putting it away as she got up on her feet, looking at the door with a hopeful look.

But to her disappointment, it was only (Y/N)'s step mother, Marilyn Thornhill.

The woman would sighed in relief, walking to Wednesday. "I didn't mean to startle you." The woman began, halting to a stop. Wednesday looked behind her, where her uncle was gone with a confused look, but shrugged it off. "I was just working on my novel." The girl began.

"Enid had requested to room with Yoko for the rest of the school year." The woman nodded at Wednesday who had a surprised look. "She did?" She questioned in disbelief, "When there's a falling out, I like to get both girls' perspectives on what happened." The woman smiled softly, "But not to mention that (Y/N) wants to move to another dorm but this one, although there is no other dorm available." The woman shrugged slightly.

"Both you and (Y/N) used to be as thick as thieves." The woman acknowledged as Wednesday's dark eyes looked at the ground slightly, "Ultimately, thieves turn on each other. I've seen it with my own eyes." Wednesday began walking from the woman to where (Y/N)'s luggage was.

"Deflect all you want," The woman began as Wednesday turned on her heel to face the lady who stood there continuing, "But you and I both know that you care about (Y/N)." The woman smiled as Wednesday's eyes widened slightly. "And you have to admit, she managed to bring out a spark of warmth in you."

Wednesday looked at the woman with an uncomfortable look as she quickly noticed, "Oh don't worry, just a tiny spark." The woman pinched her thumb and index finger together as Wednesday looked down to the ground once more. "Barely perceptible to the human eye," The woman rambled, "But, I noticed." The woman smiled, walking up to Wednesday as the pig-tailed haired girl stayed quiet.

"The part of the dorm experience is making friends with people that you wouldn't normally connect with." The lady smiled, "And those friendships often turn into lifelong bonds." She continued. "I'd rather buy a rope." Wednesday crossed her arms, and spat out bitterly to Marilyn.

"Is it really difficult for you to admit that you made a friend, and now she's gone you might actually miss her?" Miss Thornhill began, as Wednesday's eyes were fixated on the ground, a look of mixed emotions swirled in her eyes.

"I'll survive alone." Wednesday muttered, looking at the lady with a dead look on her face. "I always have." Wednesday finished.

"And as for Enid, same answer?" Marilyn stiffled a chuckle as Wednesday nodded, her eyes, now dull.

Well, if that's your decision, I'll submit the forms to Principal Weems." The woman smiled before leaving the quiet dormitory. Wednesday let out an exasperated sigh, as she wandered around the room, "Uncle Fester?" She called out, looking behind her as she heard a small squeak coming from a stuffed animal, making her turn around.

Wednesday looked at the toy for a moment, before walking to where it once was before. "Uncle Fester?" She called once more, a small giggle could be heard as she grabbed onto a fluffy stuffed bunny. To her surprise, her uncle was chilling amongst the stuffed animals. "Hey!" He yelled, startling Wednesday, "Being a solo lobo has it perks." He began, "You get to live by your own rules, do whatever you want." The man smiled heartedly.

"Just look at me!" He chortled lightly, as Wednesday dropped the stuffed animal, walking to her side of the room.

(Y/N) was walking to her art studio, her mind clouded by a phone call as she walked forward, a look of uneasiness washing on her face.

"Hi. Um, I need to talk to you." (Y/N) called, her fingers fidgeting each other, "No-- Like-- Like right now--" (Y/N) stammered slightly, her hands digging into her pocket, as she turned around. "Yeah-- Sure-- I know where that is." (Y/N) huffed, "Okay, can I meet you there in 20 minutes?" (Y/N) questioned, "Okay-- Bye." (Y/N) hung up as she turned behind her jolting at the sight of Wednesday.

"Who're you talking too?" Wednesday asked, "It's none of your goddamn business, Wednesday--" (Y/N) stuttered, a hint of irritation washing over her face. "I know what you are, (Y/N)." She taunted with a small smirk of her own. "Can you stay the hell away from me?--" (Y/N) grumbled under her breath, brushing past Wednesday to go inside her art studio.

What seemed like a few minutes, (Y/N) walked to her black ford, and slammed the door shut, starting the engine, beginning to drive to where her destination is.

(Y/N) for one, didn't see Wednesday nor her uncle stalking her.

(Y/N) was driving along the road at a fast pace, until she eventually spotted a white car in the distance halting her to a stop. She turned off the engine, and stepped out of her car and locked it behind her, walking up to the car.

"Hey! What's so urgent?" A distance voice called as (Y/N) approached the vehicle, "What happened?" The voice continued as (Y/N) stood in front of the passengers door, as out came the familiar Therapist, Valerie Kinbott. "I had a dream where you died." (Y/N) looked down defeated as the woman scoffed.

"Get in the car." She shook her head as (Y/N) put her keys in her pocket as she obeyed what the woman said, Wednesday and her uncle watching in the distance as the door slammed shut until it eventually drove away.

(Y/N) was talking with her therapist, Dr. Valerie Kinbott as the two talked to each other in the car, until she eventually pulled over at the Weathervane. "(Y/N), I have an appointment right now at the Nevermore Academy, and I do know your schedule so I'll leave you here." The woman began, as Pluto looked at the woman with an uneasy feeling, "Uh-- Thank you, Miss." (Y/N) thanked before opening up the door and making her way inside the café, waving as she walked in.

(Y/N) intentionally was doing her job, as always. Brewing coffee for the customers that came in, and out. The cycle was endless. She was too busy clouded with work that she didn't realize that time had gone fast, or that Wednesday was in the shop, watching her every move.

Wednesday was snapped out of her intense gaze when (Y/N) approached the two holding onto a small white coffee cup, "I didn't know stalking was apart of your expertise." (Y/N) pressed her lips into a thin line, sarcasm clearly laced in her voice, line with a hint of irritation, sliding the cup onto the table, "Tyler wants a word you also, since he's on break." (Y/N) acknowledge, before shaking her head and leaving the two there, as (Y/N) brushed passed Tyler in the mean time, but Wednesday couldn't help but look at (Y/N) who didn't look like herself in the distance, as Tyler and the girl talked about rescheduling their date.

(Y/N) unfortunately had to stay at the Weathervane until 11pm, which she didn't mind, it was just unexpected. (Y/N) tiredly called Xavier since her car was near her art studio from earlier at the Academy, and told him if he could pick her up. He thankfully was awake at that time and managed to pick her up.

(Y/N) walked back to her now-shared-dormitory all sluggish and exhausted as she opened the door with a creak. "What the fuck?" (Y/N) muttered aloud as she looked at the scattered papers along the floor. The room was a total mess. (Y/N) grew worried as she uttered out, "Wednesday?" She continued, "Thing?"

(Y/N)'s worried eyes skimmed all over the room as she looked at a beam on Wednesday's side of the room as it was covered in red substance. (Y/N) hesitantly but curiously walked up to it and gently put her index finger on it, as she looked at it rubbing it with her thumb and her index and middle finger.

"What is this--" She stammered skeptically, as she looked down at a knife of some sort, bending down to pick it up with her mechanical hand, examining it with wide eyes, until she realized, it wasn't a joke after all.

"Holy shit--" (Y/N) yelped in disbelief walking backwards, eventually tripping over her own feet. "Wednesday!?" (Y/N) yelled, her hands shaking, "Wednesday-- Where are you?" (Y/N)'s eyes widened as she stood up on her feet. "Please-- You must be here somewhere--" (Y/N) shuddered at the feeling of Wednesday being endangered.

(Y/N) opened Wednesday's closet to see nothing but pile of clothes and paper scattered in there. (Y/N)'s eyes fell on the ground feeling useless. (Y/N) placed her hand on her fore head slumping on the ground with a saddened look, tears beginning to brim in her eyes as she then heard faint steps coming near their dormitory doors.

"(Y/N)?" Wednesday questioned, her eyes widening as (Y/N)'s eyes immediately shot up, her eyes clashing with Wednesday's as (Y/N) immediately sprung to her feet in shock. "What-- What happened--" (Y/N) uttered, her eyes widening in terror at Wednesday, as Wednesday's eyes widened then turned into a stone-cold glare.

(Y/N) immediately ran up to Wednesday, examining her, "Are you hurt?!" (Y/N)'s voice trembled in fear.

"You did this." She determined as she stormed up to (Y/N). "You did this, I know you did." Wednesday assumed, jabbing her black-painted index finger on (Y/N)'s chest, (Y/N) noticing that tears glossed in Wednesday's eyes. "What do you mean?--" (Y/N) questioned, her eyebrows furrowed together as Wednesday's eyes threatened to spill out tears, "This-- This was all *your* fault!" She yelled at (Y/N) making her flinch.

"Woah-- Woah, Wednesday--" (Y/N) tried prying Wednesday her off. "You need to calm down--" (Y/N) ushered, "There's *nothing* that'll make me calm down." The girl glared making (Y/N) squint her eyes at her, "Are you serious right now--" (Y/N) questioned as Wednesday just scoffed at her, "Wednesday, you saw me. I was working my ass off." (Y/N) glared as Wednesday had wide eyes for a moment and remembered.

"Tell me what happened after we clean this mess..." (Y/N) shook her head in disbelief, with a hint of disappointment lacing in her voice, as Wednesday just stood there as (Y/N) was already using her telekinetic powers to pick up the papers that were scattered on the ground, Wednesday still had a pissed off look.

Wednesday had woken up in the morning as she had noticed that (Y/N) was gone.

(Y/N) was out in the cafeteria helping the chefs cook, since she admired cooking, although (Y/N) wasn't aloud in the back, but the chefs were alright with it.

(Y/N) was helping the chefs prepare tomorrows meal until the sun eventually fell. "Thanks for helping us, (Y/N)." A man with a thick accent thanked (Y/N) as she smiled heartedly at the chefs, "It's no worries, thanks for letting me help." (Y/N) began, taking off her white-colored apron, hanging it to where the other aprons were.

"You can come by anytime, I missed our cooking sessions." The woman began, placing a gentle had on her shoulder as (Y/N) chuckled, "Same here, It's busy nowadays with work and all." (Y/N) shrugged, "I'll make sure to drop by later." (Y/N) began, putting on her droopy (F/C) trench coat.

(Y/N) eventually bid farewell to them with a small smile, shoving her hands into the pocket of her coat, beginning to make her way to her Art Studio.

The dead trees and grass didn't make it better for (Y/N), as bitter-cold frost and fog hovered around the area, as she slowly approached the Art Studio. (Y/N) opened the door, closing it behind her.

(Y/N) took off her brown coat, placing it aside as flour was covered on her hoodie, as she flicked on the lights.

(Y/N) flinched when she saw the familiar black-haired girl sit on the chair, holding onto a knife that (Y/N) held the night before. "You know what-- You need to stay out of my space." (Y/N) shook her head, dusting some of the flour off herself with a heavy sigh. "Way to kill my fucking mood." (Y/N) muttered to herself as she placed her hands on her hip and raised an eyebrow. "You need to take your own advice." Wednesday glared as (Y/N) sighed, shaking her head, her arms dropping down as Wednesday jabbed the knife down.

"You left that in my room." She began, standing up to face (Y/N) who stood there, "You mean *our* dorm?" (Y/N) held a fake sarcastic smile, before it dropped making her glare. "Besides, that shit ain't mine." (Y/N) rolled her eyes.

"Actually, you left it in Thing." She proclaimed as (Y/N)'s eyebrows furrowed, "Does that explain the red substance?" (Y/N) asked as Wednesday just glared at her, continuing, "How long have you been seeing Kinbott?" She questioned making (Y/N)'s eyes widen. "Have you--" She stammered, "What am I saying-- Of course you have. You've been spying on me, right?" (Y/N) questioned as Wednesday kept quiet, still glaring daggers into (Y/N).

(Y/N) picked up the knife and examined it, her eyes filled with nothingness, "'Cause I'm the Villian in your fantasy." (Y/N) scoffed lightly, "And to answer your question, I've just been seeing her since the Harvest Festival." (Y/N) glared, the knife still in her hand.

"I was working until 11pm last night." (Y/N) scowled, "Believe me, or don't believe me." (Y/N) muttered to Wednesday. "I don't care." She whispered, as the two of the girl's face were centimeters close to each other as Wednesday backed off, slightly intimidated as she walked near (Y/N)'s newest canvas, her arms crossing.

"Your painting's been improving," Wednesday began, standing next to a particular one, "I enjoy this one in particular." Wednesday uttered, ripping off the sheet that revealed a painting of Dr. Valerie Kinbott herself, claws scratched within her face.

"Feels like you really lived it," Wednesday taunted, "What do you want?" (Y/N) sighed with a tiresome look, "I'm asking the questions." Wednesday began, turning her back toward (Y/N) as she walked to her desk, pulling out various objects that didn't belong to her.

"What is Rowan's inhaler doing in your shed?" Wednesday asked making (Y/N)'s eyes widen, "What-- ?" (Y/N) uttered a whisper, "Or Eugene's Glasses." Wednesday grabbed, "Whoa, whoa," (Y/N) began, her arm extended out, "Or these stalker images you took of me?" Wednesday began, throwing the multiple pictures on the desk.

(Y/N) began to grow worried and confused most importantly, "No, no-- I--" Wednesday interjected (Y/N)'s statement, "Don't forget your latest addition" She began as she tipped a jar of crayons out, revealing a golden necklace with a moon crescent on it. "Kinbott's necklace." She ended, making (Y/N)'s eyes widen with tears as she noticed the slight hue of red and blue blare within the distance.

"Somebody planted that stuff there--" (Y/N) stuttered slightly, her hands shaking, walking up to Wednesday as she pointed the knife at the stuff as Sheriff Galpin immediately kicked the door open, "Freeze!" He yelled, "Drop the knife! Down on your knees!" (Y/N) obeyed, her eyes widening as she looked at Wednesday with fear.

"Cuff her." The sheriff ordered as (Y/N)'s eyes widened at Wednesday, "You have the right to remain silent," The man began, "What?--" (Y/N) stuttered as her hands were being cuffed, as she looked at the sheriff in disbelief, and then looked at Wednesday with sadness in her eyes. "Anything you say can and will be used against you in court." The man continued, as (Y/N)'s eyes flickered between the sheriff and Wednesday, as the girl smirked slightly, her eyes, empty.

"You have the right to an attorney, if you cannot afford an attorney one will be appointed" The man rambled on, his gun pointed at her, as sadness turned into pure rage. "Thanks for the help, Addams." The police officer finished, as the other was done hand-cuffing (Y/N) as she was stood up by the police officer.

"You! You *framed* me!" (Y/N) yelled unconditionally as Wednesday stood there, "I'm being set up!" (Y/N) yelled at the officer who dragged her out of there, "To think that I actually *loved* you." (Y/N) yelled at Wednesday with a growl, making her flinch as sirens would wail in the distance as (Y/N) was shoved into the cop car, she was eventually taken to court.

Wednesday entered her dorm room to see Enid back inside, unpacking her things.

"Hey." Enid began, "You're back." Wednesday stammered, "I'm gone for a few days, the place gets trashed, and Thing almost dies." Enid continued, grabbing ahold of her stuffed animal, "Someone's gotta look out for you two." She paused, looking at the stuffed animal, "And it seems like (Y/N) didn't do a good job at it." She began, as she shook her head, placing it aside.

The two of them were silent for a second, before Wednesday uttered out, "What happened to rooming with Yoko?" The girl questioned, "Yoko's great. I just decided I needed a few more boundaries." Enid smiled, grabbing ahold of duct tape handing it to Wednesday, "Skip the tape." Wednesday began, "Don't tell me Wednesday Addams is mellowing out." Enid smiled cheekily.

"Never." Wednesday began, "More like evolving." Enid placed her hands behind her back, "Well, one inch of duct tape at a time." The girl smiled slightly. "Why the sudden change of heart?" Wednesday questioned, gaining Enid's attention, "Because we work." Enid nodded, "We shouldn't, but we do." Enid shrugged, "It's like some sort of weird, friendship anomaly." Enid smiled.

"Everything you said about me is true, but I don't apologize for it. Not anymore. It's just who I am." Enid became clear of herself as Wednesday stood there for what seemed like a solid minute, "Thing said he missed you." Wednesday admitted, "I missed him too." She looked down for a moment, but smiled.

"I'm sorry about (Y/N)," Enid began, fiddling with her fingers behind her back.

"I'm not." Wednesday admitted, "She's a liar and a killer." Wednesday glared at the mention of her name. "Besides, there's nothing quite like the feeling of being proven right." Wednesday began, "Except maybe someone to share it with." Enid smiled, "Thing may have blabbed about your date with Tyler, so how'd it go?" Enid smiled, looking at Wednesday who had a taken-aback look.

"It was interrupted." Wednesday admitted, Enid smiled, her smile although her smile dropped. "My ship with you and (Y/N) is gone, perished." Enid began in a dramatic tone, wiping a fake tear.

"Oh well, I heard Tyler's working the late shift," Enid began smiling as Wednesday looked up at Enid with a twinge of hope.

Wednesday walked to the Weathervane as she saw Tyler sweep up the dim-lit café. Wednesday went inside, the bell ringing slightly as Tyler called out, "We're closed." He swept.

"Then you should lock your doors." She began, as Tyler quickly perked up at the familiar voice. "There's some real sick people out there." Wednesday began, "Yeah, my dad told me what happened with (Y/N)." Tyler stammered.

"Pretty nuts." Tyler shrugged, beginning to walk toward Wednesday. "(Y/N) always seemed so normal" Tyler ranted on, "You know, for an outcast."

"Well, you know, it has made me re-evaluate things." Wednesday began, brushing past Tyler, with a dead look on her face. "Like what?" He questioned, as Wednesday turned around. "Like who I can trust." She admitted, "That mean you're ready to be more than friends?" Tyler questioned as Wednesday looked down for a moment, but then looked up at Tyler, stepping closer to him.

Wednesday then willingly placed a kiss upon Tyler's soft lips, before having another erratic vision.

Wednesday had a vision of Tyler killing Dr. Kinbott, as she immediately snapped out of her trance, in the arms of a murderer.

"Whoa-- Hey--" He muttered, "You okay?" Tyler questioned, eyes fill of concern, "I need to go." Wednesday began, rushing out of there, ignoring Tyler's pleas.

Wednesday never knew that Tyler, the one she'd nearly fallen head over heels with would be a psychotic, serial-killing monster.

Chapter Eight, A Murder full of Woes.

3RD PERSON'S POINT OF VIEW.

Enid found out that (Y/N) had escaped from prison, the night before Wednesday was nearly charged for holding Tyler hostage and nearly murdering him.

"Holy shit--" Enid babbled out, as she was helping Wednesday packing her stuff, as she got distracted and looked on her phone. "(Y/N) escaped prison--" Enid managed to utter, as Wednesday looked at Enid with a puzzled expression, "I know. I heard." Wednesday shrugged, as she looked at her ruby ring for a moment, before tearing it off and throwing it across Enid's side of the room, as the blonde haired girl hadn't notice.

The two talked to each other, until Enid had mentioned that she got a message from Eugene's mom's last night, that he woke up, until they all eventually left.

Wednesday walked down the stairs with her bags, walking up to Bianca and a few others, "The plan wasn't to get you expelled, we're sorry." Bianca apologized, "And also hearing news that (Y/N) escaped, we'll keep our ears pierced." The male siren acknowledged with a hesitant nod.

"The Nightshades need to be ready for what's coming." Wednesday alerted, "Or a lot of people are going to die." She warned, making the Nightshades look among each other with curiosity and worry.

"I'm so glad I caught you," A woman with red hair came into view, "I was weeding my wolfsbane and I just completely lost track of time." The woman chuckled slightly, "This is a parting gift," The woman began, giving the plant to Wednesday.

"White oleander, one of nature's most deadliest." Wednesday examined, "It also symbolizes destiny and renewal." The woman nodded, "You're a very talented young woman, Wednesday."

"I can't wait to see what you do next." The woman smiled, "Wednesday!" another woman's voice appeared, "This time I'm personally escorting you to your train." Principal Weems smiled, "I have one final favor." Wednesday acknowledged, owning a sour face from Larissa Weems.

Wednesday walked into the hospital room Eugene was in with a weary sigh. "Wednesday!" The boy smiled, "Eugene." Wednesday walked forward, "Glad to see you're finally awake." Wednesday acknowledged walking to the boy.

"I heard you visited all the time." The boy smiled cheekily, "Don't ever mention it again." She warned, "Listen, I've been meaning to tell you..." She paused, slightly hesitant, "I shouldn't have gone to the dance." She began, "I should have been with you." She looked down slightly, "When the dance floor calls, you gotta answer." The boy shrugged with a pained chuckle, "It's not your fault. It's the monster's." The boy sighed, "It's actually called a Hyde." Wednesday stammered.

"It's still out there. You can't go back to Nevermore, not even to check on your bees." Wednesday alerted, "And you have to listen to me this time." Wednesday warned, "I thought hummers were supposed to stick together." The boy kept quiet, recalling his memories.

"That night, in the woods." He stammered, "Someone set fire to that cave." He sighed, "Yes, Dr. Kinbott." The girl nodded, "It's so crazy that it was her." He shook his head, "I don't really remember any of it." He tried to recall, "I just saw someone wearing black, and those boots." Wednesday looked down for a moment, "What about her boots?" She began, her eyebrows creasing.

"There was an explosion of light," He flickered his fingers, making it look like an explosion, "And just for a moment," He continued, "I saw that they weren't black." he paused, "They were red." Wednesday's eyes widened in realization, that her theories were all inaccurate.

Marilyn was taking small examples of what looked like Nightshade poison, as she examined it. She then jolted and turned around her as she heard the door close. "Wednesday--" Her eyes widened, "I thought you'd be halfway across New Jersey by now--" The woman stuttered. "You can drop the act, Laurel." Wednesday glared, "I should have known it was you." Wednesday gritted her teeth.

"Faking your death, securing a job at Nevermore, unlocking a Hyde." She paused for a moment, before realization hit her, "Taking in a falsely accused prisoner." She glared, "Typically, I have a great administration for well-executed revenge plots." Wednesday continued, "But yours was a bit extreme, even for my high standards."

"Oh, dear." The woman shook her head, "Weems was right." The woman looked down and turned around, grabbing ahold of her tray of nightshade, of which had a syringe filled with the liquid itself. "You need psychiatric help." The woman began, "Can't throw away wild accusations without consequences." She turned around after placing the tray.

"They may be wild... They're true." Wednesday accused menacingly taunting her, "Tyler told me everything." Wednesday acknowledged, as she turned behind her, seeing the sickening image of Tyler walk behind her.

"You know, initially I incorrectly accused Kinbott of using hypnosis to unlock him, but you used a plant-derived chemical, didn't you?" Wednesday taunted as the woman scoffed in disbelief, "I know your father kept tabs on all the outcasts in town." Wednesday continued, "So I assumed he told you about the Galpin family secret when you were just a little girl."

"That's why you targeted Tyler."

"You manipulated him by showing him what his mother truly was."

"What Tyler didn't realize is that the truth wouldn't free him."

"It would enslave him to you."

"That was scary at first, so you used the cave and shackles."

"But eventually he willingly became your servant."

"And when Kinbott came close to discovering the truth,"

"You had Tyler kill her and pin it on (Y/N)..."

"So-- So that she can become enraged at me-- and-- who knows where she is now." Wednesday grumbled under her breath.

"Ugh. That's enough." The woman began, taking off her glasses, placing them aside. "Why would you care?" The woman glared at Wednesday, and then looked at the teenager behind her. "Tyler, Honey. Make mama happy and shut her up." She leaned against the desk, "Permanently." She determined, as Tyler flinched slightly.

"He's not on your side." Wednesday determined, "Tyler, let alone (Y/N). Will do anything for me." She brushed passed Wednesday beginning to walk up to the teenager, "Remember what I told you?" The woman questioned, "I showed you who you really are." She approached the boy, her finger tips brushed along his cheeks and jawline.

"What they did to your mother." She continued, "The outcasts made you a monster." She whispered tauntingly, putting her hands on his shoulders. "If he only hates outcasts, why is he not killing normies as well?" Wednesday questioned, "They're just pawns in a bigger game." The woman smiled menacingly.

"Just like you, Wednesday." The woman whispered to Wednesday, beginning to walk forward to her, until she eventually stopped. "Once again you've underestimated the situation, I sent Tyler there in intercept you." the girl looked at Laurel, "I never made it on the train." She then looked up toward Tyler. "Heard enough?" Wednesday questioned, as the woman looked back with terror, seeing the Principal stand there in shock and in disbelief.

"Your slave is probably still at the station." Wednesday finished.

"Please don't make this difficult than it already is, Marilyn." Principal Weems managed to utter out.

"Where. Is. (Y/N)." Wednesday glared up at Marilyn as The woman's eyes widened, ignoring Wednesday's question.

"My name is LAUREL!" The red-haired woman yelled, plunging the teal-colored syringe in her neck, as the woman dropped dead on the ground, making Wednesday's eyes widen in terror as Larissa's mouth foamed.

The woman gasped for air as Wednesday rushed to her side, "Principal Weems, Principal Weems!" The girl repeated, as the woman once known as Laurel looked at the stiff body, her eyes darkening with pure evil.

"And to answer your question, Wednesday." The woman smiled menacingly, snapping her fingers twice as a huge gust of wind came swirling around the area, as soon appeared a tall and noticeable appearance could be seen in the middle of the room, with piercing mixed hypnotized dull eyes.

"(Y/N)." Wednesday whispered, her eyes widening with tears, until she looked to her left, getting knocked out by the woman herself, as all that Wednesday saw left before getting knocked out was a cunning smile from the (H/C) haired girl herself, Pluto.

(What had happened)

As the night fell, (Y/N) awaited until the place was empty, and managed to use her telekinetic powers to release her from the dreadful, cold, and damp prison cell, managing to flee its walls.

(Y/N) immediately ran to her step mother's house, flying in the process to not attract any attention, knowing that she would've been all over the media by now. (Y/N) immediately banged on her step-mother's door, "Help me, Mother!" The girl begged, eyes fill with dread and agony.

The red-haired woman immediately opened the door, to see her step daughter teary-eyed and crash onto the wooden floor set out in front of her. "(Y/N)-- Who did this to you?" The woman asked with wide eyes, noticing the bags under her eyes. "Wednesday." The girl stared down at the ground with betrayal.

"It's always Wednesday." The girl cried, "You must help me!" (Y/N) begged as her step-mother's eyes widened, "I need your help..." (Y/N) cried, as the woman looked at her slightly, getting an idea. "Okay then, follow me." The woman began, placing a gentle hand on her shoulder, escorting her to the old and abandoned lab that (Y/N) was once in when she was younger.

"What is this?" (Y/N) began, her eyes widening, "(Y/N), everything will be done soon." The woman began as she swiftly placed a wet cloth under (Y/N)'s nose, as it held a strange and strong substance on it, making (Y/N)'s eyes widen as she slumped on the ground, her eyes closing in the process.

"Let's get you back on your feet." Laurel Gates proposed, slipping on medical gloves.

(Y/N) sat in front of Wednesday, her strong and piercing mixed eyes stung into her as she was hung by chains.

Wednesday's eyes immediately shot up, looking around the area, until she eventually made eye contact with (Y/N)'s mixed ones. "(Y/N)?" She muttered out a whisper as blood dropped down her cheek, wincing at the wound as (Y/N) yelped at the sudden disturbance.

Tyler then walked up beside (Y/N) as (Y/N) managed to stand up on her feet as Tyler looked at her for a moment, (Y/N) brushed passed the teenager with an empty look. "Kind of deja vu thing we got going on, huh?" Tyler's voice echoed out through the cave, "Except I won't cry and whine like a child." Wednesday seethed, "Tyler, Go wait by the boat." Laurel called out as Tyler looked at Laurel before nodding.

"Yes." Wednesday began, "Listen to your master and be a good little Hyde." Wednesday taunted, as Laurel approached Wednesday, Tyler nudging Wednesday before he walked out. "I must admit, that shapeshifting stunt with Weems almost worked." Marilyn uttered, "But as my father always said, If you want to out-smart an outcast, you got to out-think 'em." She smiled cockily.

"You know," Laurel began, grabbing onto a hammer, "We've got roots that go all the way out to Joseph Crackstone." The woman began as (Y/N) stood in front of

Wednesday, her dead red eyes on the ground, "Too bad he's dead." She began, wacking (Y/N) at the back of her head, making her knocked out cold on the ground, which made Wednesday's eyes widen fearful for the girl.

"(Y/N)--" She uttered out in fear, her eyes widening, "Now, now, Wednesday. You don't want to end up like her, again." The woman smiled with a chuckle, stepping over (Y/N)'s body, walking forward to Wednesday. "So you come from a line of serial killers too." Wednesday stung back bitterly, "Joesph Crackstone was a visionary, dedicating to protecting normies from outcasts, until his life was cut short." The woman walked up to Wednesday angrily.

"By your ancestor, Goody Addams." The woman shouted, "And then, to add insult to injury, they stole his land to build that abomination of a school." The woman looked down angrily as Wednesday's eyes widened, but she then soon smirked, "You mean that one you knocked out cold?" Wednesday darted to eyes down, "What do you mean?" The woman scoffed eagerly, "You gave (Y/N) unthinkable powers," The girl taunted.

"The girl to whom is a descendant of the one who killed Joseph Crackstone." Wednesday paused with a wicked smile, "Your step-daughter."

The woman shook her head, "Yeah, right." The woman scoffed, "You're just afraid to admit what your ancestor,

Goody Addams did." The woman continued, placing the lid upon the jar that contained a human face in it. "Although, throughout the centuries, my family has remained committed to Crackstone's mission." The woman sighed.

Wednesday looked down in realization that Goody Addams took the blame for Astoria's blood stained fingers, the book within Laurel's hands rightfully belonged to Astoria herself.

"My brother died serving that cause." The woman continued, "I decided to take a different approach." She paused, "The supernatural." The woman concluded, "Tyler's been collecting body parts to resurrect Crackstone." Wednesday paused, looking at the woman.

"The one man who nearly succeeded in eradicating the outcasts. "You can't wake the dead." Wednesday acknowledged, "Believe me, I've tried." Wednesday growled, "I believe your ancestor, Goody Addams, would disagree." The woman began, holding onto a thick and relevant book.

Wednesday shook her head once more, staying quiet as Wednesday's eyes widened as a small gust of wind washed over (Y/N)'s body, alarming Wednesday as (Y/N) disappeared fading into nothing but dust. "(Y/N)!--" The girl exclaimed, grunting in the process, "What have you done to her." Wednesday glared as the woman scoffed, then shrugged, "It's not like you, nor I *truly* care." The woman scoffed, as Wednesday continued to glare.

"Look, I don't know." The woman shook her head with a scoff.

"Although, I do know for a fact that Goody Addams and Astoria (L/N) were once acquaintances." The woman began, looking down onto the ground. "You're the one that stole the original from pilgrim world." Wednesday creased her eyebrows, "It wasn't enough for, well. Goody to kill Crackstone." The woman examined the thick book within her hands.

"She had to curse his soul too." Laurel began, "What does this have to do with me?" Wednesday questioned as she grunted. "My dear, Wednesday." The woman smiled, "You are the key." The woman smiled. "Your arrival at Nevermore set the chubby wheels of my plan in motion." The woman continued, "And since Goody's dear friend, Astoria was a vampire, she couldn't deliver blood." The woman began, "So Goody sealed Crackstone in his sarcophagus with a blood lock." The woman paused.

"Only one of her direct descendants can open it." The woman began, "A living descendant on the night of a blood moon." She continued, "So I bided my time, and I made you feel special." She began, "Along with my *step-daughter*, (Y/N)." She began, her voice was in a high-cocky voice. "Until you were ready to be sacrificed." She smiled.

(Y/N) cowered in fear within her inner conscience, surrounded with nothing, but the darkness that tormented her, mentally and somewhat physically.

She tried calling out to anyone beyond her reach, but couldn't seem to contact or talk to anyone. Her powers didn't work, she was technically human. She felt like her younger self. Being powerless.

It felt like days, weeks, months or possibly *years*.

She couldn't do anything, and it felt like it too.

(Y/N) wrapped herself in a ball, fear getting the best of her as tears streamed down her cheeks, the girl then heard a faint rustling noise behind her, making her look behind her within the void with wide eyes. "Who's there?" (Y/N) called out, "Can anyone help me?" (Y/N) stuttered, her eyes red from crying.

"Hello?" Her voice echoed, hesitantly standing on her feet, shaken up in fear.

"(Y/N)." An eerie voice called out, with a strained chuckle.

"They call you a tiger, but you're nothing but a mutt." The voice tormented her, a small chuckle coming out.

"Who are you?" (Y/N) yelled aloud, turning all around her in fear. "Show yourself!" The girl demanded, as an icy cold hand was placed upon her shoulder, which made (Y/N) shriek as she turned around her.

"(Y/N) (M/N) (L/N)." A voice so calming and soothing called behind her as (Y/N) yelped at the touch, turning behind her, being met with those familiar scarlet colored eyes. "Who are you...?" (Y/N) questioned, seemingly to have forgotten all about Astoria, examining the taller girl by a few inches.

The girl grinned menacingly, "Why it is I, Astoria." The girl began, as (Y/N) still had a shocked expression. "Astoria--" Astoria's smile fell, "You know-- Astoria Lela (L/N)--" Astoria began, making the girl scoff. "Don't tell me you forgot about me." The girl glared with her piercing red eyes.

"Uh... I think so?" (Y/N) questioned, slightly hesitant.

The red-eyed girl smacked her lips, "Tsk, Tsk, Tsk." The girl shook her head, "Forgetting your anscestor is one thing that ought to be done." The girl taunted with a smirk.

"What about your lover, hm?" The girl leaned in close with a taunting grin, as if she were the Cheshire cat, making (Y/N)'s eyes widen.

"Lover?" (Y/N) questioned, "What do you mean 'Lover'?" The girl questioned, as Astoria cockily crossed her arms, "Well I'm not so sure." The girl smirked, "You tell me." The girl floated in a relaxing pose, her hands resting under her chin, "Oh wait, you can't." The girl smiled, disappearing making (Y/N)'s eyes widen.

"Wait-- Please come back--" (Y/N) begged, "I'm sorry for being such an idiot earlier--" (Y/N) muttered, clear enough for Astoria to hear as she was lurking. "Just please help me." (Y/N) begged, her eyes threatening with tears as they fell on the ground. (Y/N) eventually fell on her knees, beginning to cry again, as she got no answer from her 'ancestor' she assumed.

Until a slight scoff was heard as she looked up at Astoria's dead red eyes.

"Get up." The girl scowled slightly, as (Y/N) looked at her with wide eyes for a moment as Astoria's offered her a hand as (Y/N) stayed silent for a solid minute. "Well-- Hello? What are you waiting for." The girl scowled as (Y/N) hesitantly took her warm hand into her icy ones.

"Once you go back to your human form, you'll eventually gain both your powers, and your memories." Astoria began, taking her hand back to her side. "But since your mind and body are at stake." Astoria sighed. "That is why I have come here." Astoria nodded, "Your arm is blessed by a powerful talisman." Astoria managed to utter out, as (Y/N) looked at her with a weirded-out expression.

"It'll allow me to pass through you, and heal you." The girl continued, looking at the ground, "And it'll also allow me for you to receive my powers." The girl looked at the ground hesitant for a moment as the girl placed her hands on her shoulders. "My powers are much powerful than you think." The girl with a wicked grin, "You must not get in a vulnerable state." Astoria warned.

"Just bare with me." The girl began as she looked down at (Y/N) who had wide eyes.

"You must stop Joseph Crackstone, (Y/N)." The girl began, "Avenge Wednesday for me, please." Astoria stammered.

"Because once I pass through you, you will never see me again." Astoria began as she looked at (Y/N) with worried eyes as (Y/N) just nodded hesitantly, "I'll cherish your powers." (Y/N) paused before looking down, "And supposedly my lover." (Y/N) sighed slightly dumfounded.

Astoria looked down at her with a soft sad smile as Astoria walked into (Y/N).

(Y/N) woke up in an unfamiliar area as she regained all of her memories again. "Wednesday..." that was the first word Pluto said, "Wednesday!" The girl yelped out of the hospital bed the laid in as she grunted, as her eyes widened at the familiar place.

"Why the fuck am I here--" (Y/N)'s eyes widened, "I need to get out of this place..." (Y/N) muttered to herself, as she quickly scrambled to her feet. (Y/N) then looked at her hands for a moment, before noticing the powers that she might hold.

(Y/N) flicked her hands out, as a huge gust of wind swirled around her, thinking of her destination to go, she thought about going to Wednesday.

(Y/N) thought Wednesday would be safe and sound inside her dormitory, but boy oh boy was she wrong.

(Y/N)'s soft expression turned into a look of dread and terror as it seethed throughout her. "WEDNESDAY!" The girl yelled as she ran to the girl who was on the brink of death, crashing next to Wednesday as (Y/N) placed her head on her thighs. "Wednesday..." The girl cried as she noticed that the girl unresponsive.

(Y/N) held onto Wednesday, her arms trembling as she does so as tears rolled down her cheeks.

(Y/N) plunged out the knife, her robotic hand keeping pressure on it. "No, no. Please don't do this to me." (Y/N) cried out loud, as Wednesday's eyes were truly dead.

(Y/N) cradled Wednesday in her arms, muttering to the dark haired girl, "Please don't leave me." repetitively.

Until (Y/N) realized, Wednesday was dead.

(Y/N)'s lips trembled, her hands shaking as tears of sadness turned into frustration and finally anger.

(Y/N) yelled in agony, noticing that the one of who she loved has died, as she immediately was conflicted with rage, her eyes changing into a blood shot color like her ancestors one, vowing herself, that whoever did this, shall die, no matter who or what they were.

(Y/N) left Wednesday's stiff body there as she floated up in anger, floating out the door, slamming it shut as she didn't notice that Wednesday was alive by the help of her ancestor, Goody Addams several minutes later.

(Y/N) was blinded by rage, and everything that you could think off.

(Y/N) hastily floated within the woods, hearing faint noises within it as (Y/N) picked up a certain scent from earlier as she gritted her teeth together.

Before anything could happen, (Y/N) teleported to where the noise was coming from, as she saw the Hyde, also known as Tyler, about to strike someone she couldn't see from the angle she was in.

(Y/N) reached her arm out, and used her telekinetic powers to snap Tyler's arm as he let out a strained roar, as (Y/N)'s eyes still glowed red with fury. Tyler then looked behind her with anger burning in his eyes as (Y/N) just grinned menacingly.

"Let's see who's powerful now." (Y/N) taunted as she examined his every move, dodging him, and also blocking him as she taunted him and tired him out.

(Y/N) grinned evilly, her powers getting the best of her as she did everything that could make him tire out, which worked for a small period of time.

"(Y/N)!" Wednesday yelled in the distance, as (Y/N) stopped, her eyes softening and flickering back to her normal color, but didn't worth nonetheless. "Wednesday?" (Y/N) called out, her voice breaking as she landed on the ground softly as Wednesday smiled at her from the distance, her smile fading as she realized the Hyde standing behind her.

"(Y/N)! Watch out!--" The girl warned as she was near to being torn apart, that is until Enid came along and saved (Y/N).

(Y/N) looked at the werewolf, with a relieved smile. "Enid... Thank you." The girl thanked as Wednesday looked at (Y/N) and then at Enid for a moment, "I need to get back to the school!" Wednesday yelled as she ran.

"Wait-- Wait!" (Y/N) yelled running after her, but got strained to the ground by the Hyde. "Get off me you asshole--" (Y/N) strained as she glared at the monster, using her powers to fling the Hyde off her with her telekinetic powers.

Enid then slammed Tyler to the ground as (Y/N) nodded at her and then ran to where Wednesday had gone too.

The school itself to where the erratic asshole was.

Joseph Crackstone.

(Y/N) could finally hear the familiar voices within the distance as people yelled and shouted, and (Y/N) came into view with Bianca.

"Bianca!" (Y/N) panted, "Where is Wednesday!?" The girl questioned, her eyes still dark red, and serious as Bianca's eyes widened, "(Y/N) your eyes--" (Y/N) interjected her,

"Where is Wednesday--" (Y/N)'s eyes grew in worry as Bianca looked at her with wide eyes.

"I saw her go to the Quad." Bianca began, helping the people escape as (Y/N) nodded as in thanked her as she quickly flew to where the Quad was.

"Stay away from her!" A distinctive voice was heard, coming from Xavier as he shot an arrow. (Y/N) lurked on the second floor as the man stopped the arrow, aiming back at the two as (Y/N)'s eyes widened, "No!" The girl yelled, flying in front of Wednesday in slow motion, as (Y/N) was quickly structed by the arrow as she landed on the ground with a heavy thud.

"(Y/N)!--" Wednesday yelled, bending down to (Y/N)'s side. "I'm fine." (Y/N) stammered, "Xavier, go, get them out of here." (Y/N) began, her red eyes stinging into Xavier's hazel ones as he nodded, running toward the people.

(Y/N) stood up as the arrow as it had no affect on her. The man looked at her with fearful wide eyes as she stood up in front of Wednesday as the girl cowered behind her in fear. "Well isn't it Astoria Lela (L/N)." The man hissed with a gruff voice.

"It's (Y/N) to you, old man." (Y/N) glared, her words stinging him like venom.

(Y/N) stood in front of Wednesday in a protective stance with her blood-shot eyes piercing through the man as if they were lasers. "Who needs a weapon to fight with." (Y/N) death glared, ripping out the arrow, throwing it on the ground in front of him as it meant nothing.

"You hurt Wednesday" (Y/N) muttered, drawing her blood-stained hand out, "You hurt me." (Y/N) glared, seething at her hand as she growled lowly, "For that you will die." She continued as the man gasped for air, clawing at his throat with his jagged-rimmed nails.

(Y/N) lifted the man with her telekinetic powers as she walked up toward the man who gasped for air, a look of anger, and sadness washed on her face.

"Do you know how it felt?" (Y/N) questioned stammering as her eyes glow red as she clawed her hand within his chest, ripping out his heart making the man scream in pain.

"It felt like that." (Y/N) sneered, as she used her bare hand to crush his heart making the man look at her with fear.

"Yer-- Yer a demon!" The man choked out loud as he yelled as her grunted in pain, eventually evaporating in smoke in pain as (Y/N) stood there watching the man disappear with a wide grin on her face.

Wednesday cowered behind (Y/N) as the man eventually screamed in bitter pain, exploding into nothingness, which made (Y/N) have a look of satisfaction.

(Y/N) turned behind her looking at Wednesday, a look of relaxation on her face as (Y/N) then smiled with a tired sigh. (Y/N) and Wednesday looked at each other for a moment until they heard a gun noise which made (Y/N) and Wednesday immediately turn there head in that direction.

"(Y/N), honey. Make me proud and make Wednesday shut up." The woman smiled, pointing a gun at Wednesday, "Permanently, please." The woman smiled bitter-sweetly at (Y/N), as she thought that (Y/N) was still under her control as she walked forward to the two.

"You bought a gun to a sword fight," Wednesday began, "Probably the smartest thing you've done today." Wednesday scoffed cheekily, "I might not get to kill all the outcasts," The woman threatened, "But at least (Y/N) will get to kill you." The woman seethed as Wednesday's eyes widened, looking at (Y/N) as the woman scoffed out a laugh in disbelief, "Don't tell me you've been bewitched by a tiger." The woman stifled a laugh.

"How pitiful." The woman looked down as she cocked her gun, aiming it at Wednesday who had wide-eyes as (Y/N) chuckled quietly beside her.

(Y/N) then erupted into pure laughter at the woman's childish efforts.

"You're joking." (Y/N) cackled, as she raised her hand, and flicked it at the woman as a loud snapping noise was heard as Laurel fell dead onto the ground as (Y/N) glared down at the woman with her devious dark red eyes.

"Rot in hell you stupid bitch." (Y/N) scowled, as (Y/N) looked at Wednesday who had a wide-eyed expression. "(Y/N)?" The girl called out, as (Y/N) red eyes stung with sadness and dread for the girl. Pluto looked at Wednesday with sad eyes as well as Wednesday.

The two girl's looked at each other for a moment as the two of them hesitantly were about to lean in each other for a kiss, having a moment to themselves until Eugene came.

"Hey guys-- Sorry I'm late--" The boy was cut off as he saw how close (Y/N) and Wednesday were as Wednesday had a flush of red over her face as (Y/N) just pouted slightly. "Damn." (Y/N) groaned, looking to where Eugene as he shrugged, sheepishly rubbing his hand behind his neck.

(Y/N), Wednesday and Eugene eventually walked out of the Nevermore Academy.

(Y/N) and Wednesday held onto each other's hands as Wednesday looked up at (Y/N), fearful. "Are you sure you're okay?" Wednesday as (Y/N) nodded, "Of course." (Y/N) smiled, as the three of them approached the gates.

Enid immediately broke down in tears as she engulfed both Wednesday and (Y/N) into a big hug as (Y/N) sighed warmly, holding onto Enid clinging onto her. Enid sobbed into (Y/N)'s shoulder as tears and blood were practically now stained on her shirt.

The three of them pulled apart as (Y/N) looked at Wednesday for a moment as she hesitantly, but ironically threw herself on her as tears streamed down on her face at realization. "I'm the one asking if you're okay." (Y/N) sighed sadly, gripping onto her as if she were going to go away.

The cold and bitter winter eventually hit, and (Y/N) and Wednesday barely talked to one another. It was occasionally here and there, but they barely did.

Wednesday stood in front of Principal Weems' old desk as Enid approached up behind her, "I hate to admit, but I am going to miss Principal Weems." Enid sighed looked at the ground, "She could be a real pain." Wednesday admitted.

"But she was tough." Wednesday paused, "And she died for one thing, she truly loved." Wednesday began, "This school." Wednesday admitted, looking at the ground with an uncertain look as if she longed for something, which made Enid notice but shrug it off slightly.

"For that, I have an immense of respect." Wednesday began, looking at the ground with a saddened look, "She was one of us." Enid uttered, noticing her friend's state. "Okay, Wednesday. What's the matter with you?" Enid questioned with a small smile as Wednesday flinched slightly.

Wednesday hesitantly looked at Enid for a moment before sighing. "I'm sorry. It's just that--" The girl let out a dejected sigh, looking at the ground with a sad look. "It's just that me and (Y/N) haven't spoken to each other for awhile." Wednesday looked down. "I get it though. I did put her in jail." Wednesday began, looking down in sadness.

"Maybe you'll get the chance to talk to her today." Enid smiled happily before leaving, along with the pig-tailed girl herself, leaving the room.

Enid rambled on about her vacation to San Francisco as the girl looked up to (Y/N) who stood on the second floor, looking down at Wednesday with her cold blood red eyes that never seemed to turn back after the conflict with a menacing smirk as she leaned against the rails.

Wednesday eventually walked up the stairs, making her way up to (Y/N) as she stopped, looking at (Y/N). "I hear you're a free woman now." Wednesday began as Pluto smiled, "Yup. All charges dismissed." (Y/N) smiled sadly before sighing.

"Listen," (Y/N) muttered, "When I was in my Art Studio-- I said a lot of terrible things--" (Y/N) began, digging back into her pocket, "But luckily, Enid gave me back this." (Y/N) began as she handed back Wednesday's skull ring that had engraved words on it.

"And uh-- Since you probably don't have a phone-- I bought you one, so--" (Y/N) began, pulling out a small present on it, "Welcome to the 21st century, Addams." (Y/N) smiled softly, as Wednesday opened the gift "My number's in there already." (Y/N) smiled, "That's a bold move." Wednesday began, looking down with a small smirk.

"Who knows, you might be expecting me to call you." (Y/N) chuckled jokingly, as Wednesday's cheeks flushed red as (Y/N) placed her hands in her pockets. "But honestly, Wednesday." (Y/N) looked down, her smile fading. "I truly am sorry, for being over reactive." (Y/N) huffed, "I just had a lot of emotions coming through me-- and I didn't know how to react." (Y/N) began, looking down ashamed.

"It's alright, (Y/N)." Wednesday began reassuringly, "We've all been there." The girl began, looking at the ground, then at (Y/N)'s red eyes.

"Goodbye, (Y/N)." Wednesday looked down, eyes covered in sadness as she was about to leave until (Y/N) tugged onto her black trench coat. "Miss Addams," (Y/N) looked down at her menacingly, "I believe I am missing out on a certain, kiss, perhaps?" (Y/N) chuckled as Wednesday's eyes widened with a flustered look.

"I believe our moment was ruined by a certain brown-haired boy." (Y/N) scoffed at the sudden memory, folding her arms pouting in the meantime. Wednesday's ears perked up at the sudden sentence she said as Wednesday walked to her, "A sudden kiss?" Wednesday began, looking down at the ground with a soft smile on her face as (Y/N) nodded with a smirk of her own.

(Y/N) used her mechanical hand to make Wednesday raise her chin as (Y/N) smiled at the girl softly, her red dark eyes bore into Wednesday as the two leaned in.

"May I?" (Y/N) asked with a smirk on her face as Wednesday nodded, looking from her deep red eyes to her lips until eventually their lips touched as their eyes fluttered closed as the pleasant embrace.

(Y/N) pulled backwards as Wednesday gave (Y/N) a small smirk. (Y/N) couldn't help herself as the girl gently brushed Wednesday's hair behind her ear as the girl leaned in once more, placing her non-mechanical hand on Wednesday's hip.

The two of them passionately kissed for what seemed like a strong minute as (Y/N) and Wednesday pulled away.

Wednesday's cheeks was strongly dusted with a strong tint of red. (Y/N) noticed and chuckled slightly, "You should see your face." (Y/N) chuckled slightly as Wednesday's eyes widened, "I should go." Wednesday began as (Y/N) sluggishly pouted as (Y/N) placed a small kiss upon Wednesday's cheek as she blushed furiously, getting out of (Y/N)'s grasp as she immediately walked down the stairs, leaving the (H/C) haired teenager there with a grin on her face.

"Will you be here next semester, Cara Mia?" (Y/N) called out as Wednesday grumbled something under her breath, tucking a few hair stands behind her ear with a dark blush on her face, walking down the stairs, leaving (Y/N) to smile down at her, until her figure disappeared.

Wednesday sat on the car seat, enjoying the ride until she got a random message from somebody who sent her a message, along with a message that read, 'I'm watching you'

She looked out the window, curious to who her very first stalker was.

The possibilities were endless.

The End, for now at least.

Printed in Dunstable, United Kingdom